ADVANCED PRAISE

"Here is an unvarnished portrayal of one man's elevation from the streets to a dedicated leader and role model. Stylistically, the prose is rich and makes you feel like you are right there with him on the subway or philosophizing with drug dealers, inmates, family, and friends. This book is humble greatness mixed with community action. Curtis is now one of my heroes."

JESSE THISTLE, #1 international bestselling author of *From the Ashes: My Story of Being Métis, Homeless, and Finding My Way*

"If 'be the change you wish to see' was a person, it would be Curtis Carmichael. This beautiful story of pain and triumph, setbacks, and motivation, is the kind of story our world needs right now. Curtis' words will inspire and change you from the inside, so that you have the empathetic courage to do everything better on the outside."

CELINA CAESAR-CHAVANNES, MBA, national bestselling author of *Can You Hear Me Now? How I Found My Voice and Learned to Live with Passion and Purpose*

"This astonishing life journey by Curtis Carmichael left me speechless. It takes an extraordinary individual to share their story in such a vulnerable and enlightening way that makes anyone who picks up their book a better person. The trials he encountered, embraced, and flourished from will leave readers feeling inspired to tackle their own grind. *Butterflies in the Trenches* is a call to action for Canadians in a world that profoundly needs it!"

KALEB DAHLGREN, #1 national bestselling Author of *Crossroads: My Story of Tragedy and Resilience as a Humboldt Bronco*

"Read this book while stuck on the westbound train from Kennedy Station. Read this book while waiting for your clothes to get dry at the Morningside laundromat. Just read this book. Carmichael's tenacity is exactly what makes Scarborough a magical place and what makes this book a thrilling journey."

CATHERINE HERNANDEZ, author of *Scarborough* and *Crosshairs*, screenwriter of *Scarborough: The Film*, and creator of sketch comedy audio show *Imminent Disaster*

"Carmichael throws the reader in at the deep end—but the landing is soft. With careful, poignant, and powerful prose, the reader is transported through history and geography, guided by Carmichael's ability to weave anti-racist critical theory with accessible language for a diverse audience. *Butterflies in the Trenches* takes on the difficult task of being evocative, emotional, and educational all at once—and it delivers."

CICELY BELLE BLAIN, Co-Founder of Black Lives Matter
Vancouver, CEO of Bakau Consulting, and author of *Burning Sugar*

"*Butterflies in the Trenches* lifts the veil off the devastating effects of systemic racism on Black communities and will open your eyes to the Canada you thought you knew. It's a story of survival, creativity, and the journey of a remarkable young man."

CLARA HUGHES O.C., O.M., six-time Olympic medalist and
#1 national bestselling author of *Open Heart, Open Mind*

"Compelling, honest, and deeply moving, *Butterflies in the Trenches* is a powerful story of childhood, community, and hope in one of Canada's most neglected neighbourhoods. A hugely inspiring book from an author who so eloquently writes that 'To honour those we lost, we have to become the people we needed when we were younger.' Carmichael certainly has achieved that. A vital read."

JESSICA MCDIARMID, national bestselling author of *Highway of
Tears: A True Story of Racism, Indifference and the Pursuit of
Justice for Missing and Murdered Indigenous Women and Girls*

"*Butterflies in the Trenches* is honest and necessary. Curtis shares with relatable nuance why change must start at home and the difficulties in doing so. He exemplifies perseverance; his journey offers inspiration for young and old alike."

WILLIAM KAMKWAMBA, *New York Times* bestselling
author of *The Boy Who Harnessed the Wind*

"This is a brilliant book! I wish my school's young adult booklist contained a story like this: describing a time and environment I care about in high-definition detail, in an authentic voice, and with an inspiring and insightful message. And I'm not surprised this book was partly inspired by Hip-Hop because it does precisely what rap music does at its best: proudly telling our stories and delivering our wisdom. Teachers, stock up!"

SHAD (SHADRACH KABANGO), Juno Award–winning artist
and host of Netflix's *Hip-Hop Evolution*

"Poignant and powerful. This memoir is a must read for anyone who wants to better understand how systemic inequality and generational legacy work."

DONNOVAN BENNETT, award-winning producer, TV host, and radio host for *Sportsnet*

"Mr. Carmichael provides an honest autobiographical look into his life, community, struggles, and triumphs. It is heartfelt, honest, and exactly what we need at this time when confronting systemic racism has become part of the zeitgeist. Scarborough is not just a place; it is a state of mind. Mr. Carmichael wonderfully captures this duality. An insightful read!"

DR. CHERYL THOMPSON, distinguished professor of communication and media studies, Ryerson University, and author of *Uncle: Race, Nostalgia, and the Politics of Loyalty* and *Beauty in a Box: Detangling the Roots of Canada's Black Beauty Culture*

"This book is an eye opener. Capturing painful realities of growing up in a racially and economically challenged Toronto, Curtis clearly presents harsh realities as he goes through his own personal life transformation. I thank him for sharing this intimate part of himself and for introducing us to many other change makers who, like Curtis, inspire us to become our better selves."

BERNICE CARNEGIE, author of *A Fly in a Pail of Milk: The Herb Carnegie Story*

"Told with heart and honesty, Curtis takes us through an incredible dichotomy of Canadian life, makes it accessible to readers, reminds us to tell our own stories, and do our part to change the world."

MICHEL CHIKWANINE, former child soldier, international keynote speaker, and author of *Child Soldier: When Boys and Girls Are Used in War*

"*Butterflies in the Trenches* is a riveting portrait of triumph through struggle. An insight into the determination and tenacity needed to live beyond one's own potential. Each chapter is a kaleidoscope of learning; business, engineering, athletics, and culture are beautifully woven through a heartwarming and inspirational narrative. Curtis inspires all of us to sift through the sludge and find the glimmering wheels of hope carrying us towards the power within."

IAN KETEKU, World Poetry Slam Champion and author of *Black Abacus*

"Curtis has the ability to speak candidly to the systemic inequalities in public housing and in educational systems. Carmichael interrogates the challenges that Black youth must navigate while underlining the resilience and drive of his community. This book is a must-read for those not only interested in leadership, community engagement, and the power of youth, but for those who want to change the world one step, or pedal, at a time."

SHIREEN AHMED, international keynote speaker, award-winning sport activist, and columnist at *TSN*

"In this insightful, compelling memoir, Carmichael adds to his impressive list of inspiring contributions where we can learn how a young Black man navigated the structures of inequity to become an award-winning athlete, educator, and community activist."

DR. CARL E. JAMES, distinguished professor of education, Jean Augustine Chair in Education, York University, and author of *Colour Matters: Essays on the Experiences, Education, and Pursuits of Black Youth*

"Curtis is a role model to our next-gen leaders; someone who is committed to helping young adults break barriers, rules, and societal norms. This book will enlighten and guide the next steps for every dreamer, believer, doer, and thinker."

PAULEANNA REID, Founder of WritersBlok and New Girl on the Block, and bestselling author of *Everything I Couldn't Tell My Mother*

"This book fed my soul! From pain to perspective, to possibilities to purpose. Mr. Carmichael takes us on a physical, emotional, and metaphorical journey that is inspiring, energizing, and galvanizing. It left me feeling that we MUST do something, anything, and everything we can do to change the narrative. Curtis is a brilliant messenger of hope . . . and he is also the message."

ORLANDO BOWEN, professional CFL athlete and Founder and Executive Director of One Voice One Team

"As the adage goes, 'Scarborough to the world,' because, as Curtis Carmichael masterfully shows, you can paint a future of the world from this place, in all its difficult, unruly beauty. *Butterflies in the Trenches* offers us poignant images of a beloved community and its radiant lives in the making, from the voices of the hood philosophers that call this city home."

DR. ADRIAN DE LEON, distinguished professor of history, University of Southern California, and author of *Rouge*

"Great reminder that we can never judge a book by its cover, though we always have a choice of what we do; sometimes we are born into situations where we are just trying to survive by any means necessary. Curtis showed how wisdom and guidance can often come from the most unexpected places and sources if we are open enough to listen."

AKEEM HAYNES, Olympic bronze medalist, international keynote speaker, and author of *Fear, Faith & Fruition* and *Love, Life & Legacy*

"Curtis Carmichael's vivid, first-hand story of growing up in the poverty and racism of community housing in Toronto takes a remarkable turn, emerging as a practical guide for encouraging hope and fostering human potential. Anyone committed to contributing toward real progress on equity, inclusion, and social justice will find inspiration and insight in this powerful manifesto for nurturing opportunity through learning, STEM, technology, and role models."

DR. MOHAMED LACHEMI, President and Vice Chancellor of Ryerson University

"If you come from hardships and trauma, *Butterflies in the Trenches* will provide meaningful and inspirational signposts on your journey of healing. If you don't, it will open your eyes to all that a comfortable existence has hidden from you. There is true wisdom in this memoir where lived experience meets philosophy. Ultimately, it shows that if you take steps to 'become who you needed when you were younger,' if we all do, the world will be a very different and a much better place."

DR. BENOIT-ANTOINE BACON, President and Vice Chancellor of Carleton University

"Curtis Carmichael is proof that the lessons learned on the streets can transfer to the boardroom and beyond. The resilience and resourcefulness that is required for survival in the hood is a sought-after asset in the business world. He is a reminder that the great leaders of tomorrow may be living in public housing today."

ANTHONY MCLEAN, international keynote speaker, host of CBC's The X, and featured in the award-winning documentary *Colour Me*

"Curtis surprises readers with a compelling insight, thoughtful observation, and new way of looking at things. *Butterflies in the Trenches* isn't just a great story: it's a love song of hustle and motivation, but it's also a challenge to all of us to try and match Curtis' incredible example."

DR. MATT HERN, distinguished professor of urban studies and alternative education, Co-founder of Solid State Community Industries, and author of *On This Patch of Grass: City Parks on Occupied Land*

Butterflies
in the
Trenches

The Hood,
an Epic Bike Ride,
and
Finding Inspiration

Curtis
Carmichael

SYNERGY
B O O K S

Vancouver • Winnipeg • Toronto • Montreal • Halifax

SYNERGY
B O O K S

202-2149 Yonge Street
Toronto, ON M4S 0C5

First edition published 2021 by Synergy Books

Butterflies in the Trenches may be purchased for educational, business,
or sales promotional use through our Special Sales Department.
For more information about special discounts for bulk purchases,
live events, speaking engagements, or workshops, contact the
author's management team at: www.curtiscarmichael.ca

Cover design by Adrian So
Cover image by Devante Thomas/TonyTones of XVXY Photo
Interior design by Lewelin Polanco
Interior photo of Ermias Asghedom by Jerritt Clark (Getty Images)

Printed and manufactured in Canada

10 9 8 7 6 5 4 3 2 1

Library of Congress Cataloging-in-Publication Data is available.

ISBN 978-1-7776840-0-6 (Paperback)
ISBN 978-1-7776840-1-3 (Hardcover)

Butterflies in the Trenches

Although butterflies feed on the nectar of flowers, they rely on mud puddles to obtain minerals and nutrients essential to their survival and reproduction. From the mud, they safeguard their survival; the humble caterpillar crawls in the mud and emerges a butterfly. To many, the caterpillar and the butterfly are completely different. But to me, the caterpillar and butterfly are one and the same.

To all the butterflies in the trenches: keep crawling through the mud and keep flying to new heights. By any means necessary.

To my fam, the block, and those we lost along the way.

To Blue Boy, Isaiah, Adrian, Shawn C., Andre H., Ron, Stephen, Esmie, Zako, Rita, Ma, Sheila, Cherry, Pauline, Betta, Art, Alisa P., Jason S., and James P., may you rest in Power.

For T, E, Winston, and Tenisha.

More life. Forever.

Yesterday I was clever, so I wanted to change the world. Today I am wise, so I am changing myself.

—Rumi

When you learn, teach, when you get, give.

—Maya Angelou

Contents

PART 1: *Survive*

PART 2: *Transcend*

Foreword

Uncanny or poetic justice? I'm sitting down to express the depth of my passion for this heartwarming love story the day before Valentine's Day. In the spirit of transparency, I openly confess that I, the pro football Hall of Famer, am often the first one to cry out of my wife and three girls. This book doesn't offer us a traditional love story, but it's all the more inspiring for it. Our author, Curtis Carmichael, is a flourishing athlete himself. His prowess provided him an opportunity to pursue a career in professional sports. Instead, he made a promise to his first love. Awkward, given she had betrayed him more than once, but this only made her more alluring. As he watched her continue to give birth, he became even more resolute.

This love, this lady in waiting, is Scarborough; not an exotic love interest, but the community he grew up in. Returning home with a degree from the prestigious Queen's University, his world had changed, but the community that could have made him another victim had not. Empathetic, because he had walked the walk of youth in his postal code, he knew action was imperative, and so he decided to ride across Canada. That's right, he decided to traverse the second largest country in the world, from the Pacific to the Atlantic Ocean, on two wheels and no motor! This lofty goal, which became known as the Ride for

Promise, provides the backdrop for this passionate thriller of true love . . . putting his community before himself.

Curtis Carmichael's memoir, *Butterflies in the Trenches*, is about his vision in action, about using the Ride for Promise, STEM education, and entrepreneurship to break the cycle of poverty. The spark that was lit by the defunding of vital programs in Scarborough was almost extinguished by gunshots before the ride even began. A friend, gone, and Curtis' motivation temporarily neutralized. But he remembered the youth. His love and respect for the youth in his community is authentic, as was his dismay at finding his community unchanged and the overwhelming problems of the past not just still present but still prevalent. In the spirit of Gandhi, he adapted and adopted the principle of being the change you wish to see.

History, or should I say his story, reminds me of my own. So much dormant talent, not just in sports and the arts, but in engineering, invention, leadership, technology, entrepreneurship, and teaching. His riveting personal accounts of brilliance are transcendent: Dr. Alex, the kid who turned a recycled lawnmower and bicycle into a dependable motor vehicle that sufficed for affordable transportation; Dre, the recreational drugs coordinator whose further enlightenment transformed him into a wordsmith, proliferating a thirst for reading and education. Raw and real, the same guy that taught kids how to sell drugs gave Curtis his first dictionary. His encouragement was reinforced by the cadence of rhyme, "the more words you know, the higher you go!" From hustle to wholesome, Curtis unpacks it all on his ride and draws on the inspiration and life of Ermias Joseph Asghedom, known professionally as Nipsey Hussle, maybe the most iconic superstar in recent history to elevate community "inside out;" giving back to the neighbourhood where most leave and reach back or, worse yet, think back but never come back.

This literary gem speaks to hardships and heroes—it details a grueling, body-destroying ride that brought up overwhelming memories of childhood trauma and depression but also offered therapeutic conversations with friends and with communities across the country.

The daily obsession with hurt and oppression brought on depression that demanded intercession and finally progression. He pushed through once again, this time in full sight of what was behind him. I've always known there was untold excellence, unseen beauty, and brilliance without a platform in marginalized communities: *butterflies in the trenches*. I humbly admit from my suburban abode that Mr. Carmichael has also taught me that "success is not making it out, it's making your life and community better."

If you're looking for a book with an incredible ending, you're in the wrong place. This is just part one for Curtis Carmichael. This is just the beginning!

Michael Clemons

GM Toronto Argonauts
CFL and Canadian Sports Hall of Fame
Co-Founder Pinball Clemons Foundation

A Note from the Author

This book is a work of nonfiction and it explores a world rooted in injustice. The effects of this injustice are personal to me and they impact many people in my community, in neighbourhoods like mine around the world, and the people we met along the way.

Sometimes in life the only way to connect the dots is to look backwards. That's what writing this book has taught me. As you read, take care of your mind and heart. Pause, rest, and take a breather if needed. We are living in difficult times. Remember to hold onto the truth that always remains solid throughout history and the present: where there's people, there's power. Stay safe. Keep your head up. More life. One love.

Introduction

I'm back on the same corner where I hustled as a youth. Not much has changed in the last ten years. The government's legacy of underfunding our communities while somehow always finding a way to increase the policing budget and give big financial packages to large corporations continues. This is the norm on this land, in Toronto and throughout Canada. Despite mainstream narratives of "multiculturalism" and the "Glorious and Free," Canada has a long history of underfunding and over-policing low-income communities across the country, including Black and Indigenous communities and housing projects like Toronto Community Housing, which is the largest public housing provider in Canada and the second largest in North America.

Today, as a STEM and hip hop elementary teacher, Team Canada Duathlete, computer programmer, and inspirational keynote speaker, I have spoken across Canada to teachers, principals, superintendents, and leaders of big corporations and charities. But I've grown tired of being in rooms with people who wear expensive suits and disingenuous smiles, people who have a drone-like perspective on my community and others like mine but have never stepped foot on the block. They speak as if they know more about our hoods than the people who actually live there. Their words are foolish because they only speak of stereotypes and massive generalizations fed to them by the news or social media. Some of them call themselves "experts," but what they do is straight criminal.

When I was a kid, my homies and I always searched for Canadian books about growing up in Toronto or hoods across Canada. We wanted to read a nonfiction story that provided an insider's view of living in a housing project. We wanted to read about a person who broke the cycle they were born into and came back to the hood to equip others with tools to do the same. We wanted someone who gave the block free gems and useful tools about financial education, business, entrepreneurship, technology, and mental health and wellness as the world changed rapidly around us. We wanted to make some real changes in our lives and on the block so we could take care of ourselves and our family long-term. We wanted to level up by making some real money. Unfortunately, I couldn't find any books like this, so I challenged myself to write the book I was searching for.

I've always looked up to people like Terry Fox, Rick Hansen, and Nipsey Hussle. When he was only 17 years old, Terry Fox was diagnosed with osteogenic sarcoma—bone cancer—in his right leg and had the leg amputated six inches above the knee. But he had incredible drive, and he decided to run across Canada to raise money and inform Canadians about the importance of finding a cure for cancer, running an average of 42 km every day for 143 days.

Rick Hansen suffered a spinal cord injury and became a paraplegic after being in a truck accident at age 15. In a wheelchair, he completed an epic 40,000 km, 26-month journey to 34 countries across the globe to make the world inclusive for people with disabilities, find a cure for paralysis, and inspire the world to make the planet more accessible for all. As a child from the hood, these stories were inspirational but they were not connected to my block. We did not have a person like Terry or Rick, someone who came from the mud and did something for the hood on a national level. We needed someone the kids could see, touch, and learn from. So in 2017, I set out to become that person by cycling across Canada. It wasn't close to the level of Terry and Rick, but it was important for me to bring some block motivation to the hoods in Scarborough, Toronto, and throughout Canada.

In the end, my number one inspiration is the global icon Ermias Asghedom, professionally known as Nipsey Hussle or Neighbourhood Nip—"the Tupac of our generation." He was a Grammy award-winning rapper, business mogul, philanthropist, community activist, serial entrepreneur, father, and the owner of more than ten businesses and community-based programs in his neighbourhood, which included owning land and multiple real estate properties. Watching Nipsey change his life and community, going from hustling on the corner and generational gang culture to global icon, changed my entire perspective on what it meant to come from a place with few resources, where you had to create your own opportunities. Nipsey believed anything was possible and showed our communities that we have value, skills, and talents even though we have limited platforms to show our genius. He is a global model of how to invest in yourself and your community and pass power to the people in your community. He inspired me to play chess instead of checkers and use my own story as a way to help youth break out of the cycle of poverty and away from the miseducation of an education system bent on keeping us down.

After speaking across Canada to middle school and high school students at school assemblies, I realized I could help youth by telling my life story, by sharing real stories about the hidden realities of growing up in Toronto Community Housing projects. I decided to write this two-part memoir, taking readers on a journey across Canada, following my charity bike ride from beginning to end. Along the way, I share the raw stories from my childhood that were replaying in my head as I cycled coast to coast. They are the pieces of myself that I remember, not the whole story. These are the stories I can put into words, the stories that I am emotionally able to part ways with. In part one, I move back and forth between reflections from my cross-Canada cycling journey and flashbacks to my childhood and the trauma that came with growing up in poverty in the hood that were triggered as I cycled. These flashbacks give you a glimpse into my childhood, growing up in the community housing projects in Scarborough, Canada, and my evolution from a childhood drug dealer to cycling across Canada. In part two, I share stories of other Black youth from around the world who have made a difference for their communities and the world. I also reflect on what helped me break the cycle of poverty, the miseducation of the school system I was born into, and how I came to see myself and my community differently.

Unfortunately, the books I'd eventually read that helped improve my life and those around me were not accessible to me while I was in school. By writing this book, I hope to change that by speaking directly to you. I hope that you are empowered by my story of creating something from nothing and that it helps you see yourself and your community in a different light. I want you to dive deeper into the different topics that speak to you so you can also play chess rather than checkers.

This book is a written and visual storytelling of my life in Scarborough. I put this together to challenge the stigma and stereotypes of communities like mine, to show the beautiful roses in the concrete and the streets that made us. As I continue to fill the gaps and make sense of my life, I hope the stories I share touch your soul and give you a different perspective on what it means to find light in the darkness when there seems to be no hope at all.

This book is dedicated to you.

Butterflies in the Trenches Mobile Application

This book is the world's first Augmented Reality memoir. The words and photos in the book are brought to life with our own mobile app. By holding your phone over specific photos in the book, our *Butterflies in the Trenches Smart Book App* will allow you to access hidden content, including videos and interactive visual and audio content on your screen. For more information on the mobile app and download instructions for iOS, Android, or alternative viewing options, go to the mobile app page on the website: https://www.curtiscarmichael.ca/

Ride for Promise

> *Sometimes we have to do the work even though we don't yet see a glimmer on the horizon that it's actually going to be possible.*
>
> —Angela Davis

I was tired. The kind of tired that makes you want to sleep forever and maybe not wake up.

Ten years ago, I was in high school, living on my family's living room couch. Now, I was back on the same block with a piece of paper from my university and a student debt the size of a down payment on a new home. After doing everything I was told to do—go to college, get a degree—I was back to square one, living face to face with the violence that continued to steal the lives of those close to me in underfunded hoods. In nine months I was supposed to be riding across Canada, but I was on the verge of quitting before I even began. That day, my life took a turn and I learned how to channel my pain and mourning into a movement.

5:00 a.m.: *Westbound to Kipling Station*

I hopped on the train at Warden headed to Yonge Station to trek to my Saturday morning shift. The frosty November day started off in complete darkness with no fall sun in sight—the kind of weather where you can see your breath as mini clouds each time you exhale. The train was empty of humans but completely filled with zombies. I do not think anyone had woken up yet, or was going to, me included. Sitting, hoodie up—wearing all black everything—I fit my head nicely into the nook of the train window. I was praying for a 20-minute nap before I started work at the Toronto Athletic Club, an elite fitness facility on top of the Bay Street TD Tower where I was the weight room supervisor.

No train southbound to Union Station.

I sprinted to get off the train before the door jingles came to a close. I just made it. I saw the TTC service attendants in red shirts but I didn't ask questions—I knew something was up; something was out of service. I started booking it down the strip from Yonge Street to Union Station. I don't wait for the shuttle bus ever. I'd rather walk than stand chest to chest with people who woke up so early they forgot to brush. Sardine can buses were not the comfortable vibe, but you gotta do what you gotta do.

I was approaching the Eaton Centre when three buses flew right by me. Turns out they were empty. But I was between stops and wasn't trying to pull an Usain Bolt this early. There was still sleep residue in the corner of my eye and my morning breath was kicking even though I brushed. Twenty-minute naps on the TTC were deadly. They could disease your mouth again in seconds.

It was 5:45. I was two blocks away from work. I received a phone notification and stopped quickly in the nook of the bus shelter to check. I pulled out my iPhone 6 and tried not to split open my hands scrolling down on my shattered screen. False alarm. Just an app update and email notifications from deals I should have unsubscribed from after I got the discount. Without realizing it, I started mindlessly scrolling on Instagram. When I snapped back to reality, I forgot where I was and it took me a minute to realize that ten minutes had passed and I now had five minutes to get to work or I would be late. I was about to exit the app to lace up my Air Forces when a post caught my eye, then a series of posts, trending. An RIP. My childhood friend . . . shot and killed.

I went frantically to the online news and all my social accounts to see what went down. It was confirmed on social media and over text before the news station even got the scoop. Journalism in the streets by the streets was always faster at reporting. Just last evening, a car pulled up beside the whip and emptied the clip. The chrome pierced through the exterior of the car, entering his body. His life, his dreams, his fight, his smile, his laugh, his hopes and aspirations gone in a second. He didn't make it to the emergency department in time.

"Fuck!" I yelled down the empty Bay Street alleyways.

In my mind, tears were rippling down my cheeks, but externally, I seemed unphased. I hadn't cried in years. I hadn't learned how to express emotion so I stood still in the crevice of the bus shelter, frozen, before snapping back to reality. I had to get to work. It began to grate my insides—the dozens and dozens of friends and family that were stolen from us in these streets. In that moment, in my mind, I said, forget the bike trip. I lost interest in doing anything that once brought me joy.

I was reaching a turning point. At that moment, planning for the ride across Canada was not going to happen. Living in the hood, I did not have massive networks or connections like people in wealthy communities had since they were kids—they had everyone from CEOs, doctors, lawyers, inventors, politicians, engineers, celebrities, and more on speed dial. They were globally connected. On the flip side, I knew everyone in the streets. I was hood connected. I had street corner entrepreneurs on speed dial; the kind of connections that were only valid in the streets. While the richer communities had cottages and multiple homes, we were living in overcrowded apartments with couches and living room floors as substitutes for mattresses or three to four people using one queen sized bed. In the middle of an affordable housing crisis, with ten-plus years wait time for the next available public housing unit, my social capital was a different kind of currency that couldn't be used anywhere other than the block.

After the first three months of planning I reached a standstill. I had nine months to go with nothing more than my used Kijiji bike, a black and white printed map of Canada, and a play-by-play of the plan to make it happen. I had a vision of a van full of people to drive beside me as I cycled coast to coast, but I had nothing. No sponsorships, no van support team, no food for the months it would take to complete, no places to sleep and no venues picked out in the cities along the route for me to speak about my cause. All I had was a dream and my boy Addisiane who was down to do it even if we had to sleep outside with no food. He was a real one. These major losses were the proverbial nail in the bike tire that threatened to stop my movement. But what happened next saved it.

◌◌◌◌◌◌◌

I was still standing, frozen, under the bus shelter, when out of nowhere I smiled to myself as my childhood memories started to roll down my cheeks. With one droplet, which somehow squeezed itself out, I reminisced about the life of my childhood friend. He had brought the community closer by teaching everyone on the block how to do bike tricks—cat walks and wheelies—to pass the time. He was the best rider on the block and could pop a wheelie for days. Doing multiple laps of our four-city block community, he would ride forwards or backwards on one wheelie for ten minutes on his first try. He was a street legend. A legend who gave us a love for fitness and physical activity and being creative with our bikes and whatever we had in our possession. With no community programs on a hot summer evening, the bike was all you had. He was a hope that inspired us to do something else with our time instead of just being bored out of our minds standing on the corner.

We all had an emotional connection to our block because that was our home, where we celebrated our wins and carried around the losses we couldn't erase. Shell shocked sometimes when the grim reaper's phone call or text came in, you didn't answer because you knew what was on the other line.

Just when I wanted to quit on life and this movement, I thought of him. I thought of all the kids, families, parents, youth, inmates, and people who were taken from us way too young. I would be biking for them. I didn't want to be the voice for Toronto Community Housing hoods and communities alike. I just wanted to bring a different narrative and perspective than the one that was created by people who had never stepped foot in the hood but were somehow "experts," or so they nominated themselves.

If I did not bike across Canada to highlight the realities of living here under systemic racism, without resources and opportunities, I felt I would be letting down the very people I live amongst. They were counting on me. *If I didn't bike across Canada for my community, then who would?*

Inspiration

> *Sometimes people try to destroy you, precisely because they recognize your power—not because they don't see it, but because they see it and they don't want it to exist.*
>
> —bell hooks

I looked to the inspiration of Terry Fox, Rick Hansen, and Orlando Bowen and realized that when you want to quit is exactly when you need to keep going forward.

Terry Fox couldn't control all that happened to him, but he made the choice not to be defeated by those conditions. Though he was forced to stop the run on September 1, 1980, when cancer spread to his lungs, Terry achieved his dream of raising one dollar for every Canadian on February 1, 1981, raising 24.17 million dollars. In June 1981, Terry died a world hero and global icon.

Rick Hansen, bound to a wheelchair at only 15, made the choice to be on the move for social change. It was just the beginning of his new life. Inspired by his friend and Canadian athlete Terry Fox, Rick decided to undertake a similar journey with the goal of making the planet more accessible for all. In the time before social media, when there were zero likes, zero shares, and zero reposts, Terry and Rick ended up with millions of worldwide followers. But they didn't do it for the popularity, they did it for the people.

In 2004, Orlando Bowen thought he was about to die. A professional football player and CFL linebacker, Orlando was jumped by two plainclothes police officers who planted drugs on him and then pinned him to the ground and beat him violently. This act of police brutality gave Orlando a severe concussion and ended his football career, but he never gave up on his community. After being proven completely innocent, Orlando—incredibly—publicly forgave his perpetrators and dedicated his life to inspiring others to pursue excellence in all they do. In 2008, he became the founder and executive director of One Voice One Team, a youth leadership organization that empowers youth to utilize leadership skills and talents to better themselves and their community. Speaking to over 300,000 people worldwide, he continues to inspire everyone to get off the sidelines and make a difference in their lives and communities by serving others. To Orlando, making a difference for others as well as yourself is what makes you a gamechanger.

If I didn't bike across Canada for my community, I started to ask myself who would. The answer echoing in my soul and mind was *no one*. So I knew that I had to be the one. The kids on my block were looking for someone in the streets that they could see and interact with. They wanted a person who understood the struggle directly so they could see themselves fully in them. We did not have an Orlando Bowen. We did not have a Terry Fox or a Rick Hansen. But in our hood, the kids had me. While my efforts may not have gotten the kind of global fame that Terry, Rick, and Orlando did, I did do enough to bring motivation to my people, to the people who needed it most. I would call it Ride for Promise. It was a promise I made to the community. I would finish what I started.

I couldn't control the events that happened to me and around me— growing up amongst poverty, inadequate schooling, underfunded neighbourhoods, drugs, crime, violence, police brutality, shootings, all connected to systemic racism—but I could decide that I wouldn't be bullied by the circumstances of my environment. I had taken control of the controllable and released what I couldn't control.

Full Circle

Years later, thinking back to block kids building motorcycles from scratch and learning about business and entrepreneurship through drug dealing and building my own bike shop when I was 11, I realized I did not have to learn new skills to start a movement. I had to use the same skills I had developed on the block, just in a different way. I decided I would build this movement like I built my bike business and the way I and others in the streets hustled. I would use the Design Thinking process. It was simple for me. I reverse engineered my goals. I mapped out a plan beginning with the end of the bike ride in Nova Scotia then worked backwards by writing down my goals step-by-step. With a detailed plan for how to accomplish the movement, I could do small, consistent actions day by day. I did one thing at a time, including exercising, emailing, making phone calls, stretching, mailing letters, and social media outreach. For the first eight months, it was a lonely grind. No one believed in the vision but me. Not many people helped at first. People called me crazy. Many people said I was wasting my time. But after eight months of grinding, I got the ball rolling.

Once I had momentum, people wanted to join the movement by helping wherever they could, whether it was donations of money, riding equipment, or food. Others joined as I started to make some movement forward and felt like they were a part of something bigger than themselves. What was happening was a testament to the idiom: people help those who help themselves.

In the final two months before the ride began, everything was coming together. My faith in the beginning was crazy, but in the end my vision was strong enough to attract others who believed in me and the cause. When things didn't go as planned, I learned not to hold on to frustration for too long. I just went back to the drawing board with new information to make a better decision. I knew society was wrong. I wasn't a failure. I was a scientist. On my block, we were all scientists. If scientists stopped trying after a failed test or experiment, we would have zero breakthroughs in scientific discoveries. We were just experimenting, and I had to use that knowledge to become better every time I got back up to bat.

Some of the people who became my biggest supporters were the biggest haters in the beginning. These were the people who shot down the ideas before they even had a chance. I didn't forget who they were. These were the same people who said I wouldn't ever stop selling drugs. The same people who said I wouldn't stay in school, that I wouldn't be able to make the high school football team, that I wouldn't do well in school, that I wouldn't make it to university, that I wouldn't make it on to the university football team. The same people who said I wouldn't amount to anything. And they once said I wouldn't make it across Canada. I knew what I was capable of and their opinions never mattered. Looking back, I see that if I did nothing, then I would be in the same predicament I was in yesterday. My three goals for my life and the moment were to work smart not just hard, play chess not checkers, and show love to my people. It was Canada 150, the 150th anniversary of Confederation as promoted by the Canadian government in 2017. But I was not celebrating. I was cycling to challenge the very country that was rooted in systemic racism. A nation responsible for the ongoing genocide of Indigenous people, for the slavery of Africans on this land, and for the Missing and Murdered Indigenous Women and Girls—a national crisis and Canadian genocide. One of the biggest myths told to us kids in school was that Canada was a safe haven for Black people. In reality, the many who escaped slavery in the US were re-enslaved once they made it to Canada through the Underground Railroad.

The truth is that Canada is a country built on genocide and land that was stolen for profit, forcing Indigenous people onto reserves and into residential schools. The only difference between the United States and Canada was that Canada hid behind claims of "multiculturalism" and pointed a finger south of the border to avoid dealing with its own problems. People who were telling us anything different were blind to history and the conditions different communities live under. Hundreds of years later and we are still fighting the ongoing colonization that is the lifeblood of the "True North strong and free."

At the time, I had just completed my football career as a student at Queen's University. As a starting slot receiver, I gained enough national attention to get invited to the Canadian Football League Evaluation Combine to participate in physical testing in front of professional football coaches. After performing well in the 40 yard dash, broad jump, vertical jump, three cone drill, shuttle run, and the 225 bench press test, I signed with a CFL agent. I was on my way to a practice roster at least. I was small in size but mighty because I was from Scarborough.

Coming back to the hood during draft season, my life changed direction when I realized I only played football because I was good at it . . . I wasn't passionate about it. I decided to hang up my football cleats instead of pursuing the CFL. Oddly, I felt like I was exactly where I needed to be. I was more passionate about the community and cycling across Canada for the hood even though I didn't know if I would make it. I didn't have a clue what would happen next, but I was ready to cycle from Vancouver to Africville or die trying.

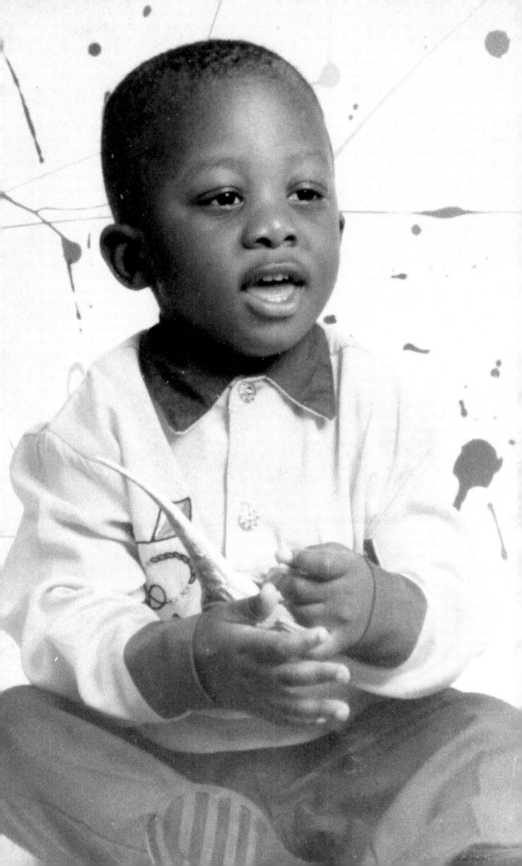

PART 1
Survive

> *The streets were not my only problem. If the streets shackled my right leg, the schools shackled my left. Fail to comprehend the streets and you gave up your body now. But fail to comprehend the schools and you gave up your body later.*
>
> **—Ta-Nehisi Coates**

Poverty is Violence

Pretty soon empty spoons cut gums
like razor blades across faces in penitentiaries
the summer of 98 took lives
off of family porches

&

out of family portraits
it also took the Jordan's off of Jermaine's feet
along with his breath
last words were "don't scuff em"

&

when people don't eat
They eat each other bone and all
I AM, staring at an empty closet
waiting for the bones to fall

&

because an empty stomach
gets filled with lucifer
we been keeping the door locked
everyday this June
the wavy apparitions rising from concrete
reminded us, summer was in

&

the heat was on

—*Tariq Touré*

Scarborough

Age seven: My mom, dad, two older brothers, and I lived in Regent Park—Canada's first and largest public housing neighbourhood—but we moved to the eastside of Toronto to the district of Scarborough when I was a kid. Spending most of my childhood in the Scarborough community, I was a product of the east end.

What Queens is to New York is what Scarborough is to Toronto. Our neighbourhood was in the middle of the bushes, a thickly forested valley surrounding Massey Creek, with trees hugging each corner of the block; this forest was known as Warden Woods. If you travelled on the subway train eastbound to Kennedy Station, you would see sunlight for a few brief minutes between the station stops of Victoria Park and Warden before going back underground. That sunlight was our neighbourhood. Eastside across the tracks from Teesdale was my neighbourhood, called Block 13, which included Cataraqui, Firvalley, 680, and Southside located in the southwest region of Scarborough. This was my home. I was only seven, but I learned to rep my block everywhere I travelled. What I loved most about this side of the city wasn't only how easy it was to sneak into Warden subway station to snag one of the best subway station beef patties in the city—it was dope because of the people.

In neighbourhoods full of colour, literal colour, representing each region in Africa, every country around the Middle East, a tiny percentage from Europe, and predominantly, the African diaspora from the Caribbean, our neighbourhood melanin was popping. We were everyday people who didn't make the news or appear on TV. There were families, many of whom were hard working immigrants, working a million jobs to secure the bag, and some were mom and pop shop business owners. Our communities were filled with a vibrance of culture and tradition, the best, most seasoned food in the city, dope art and community spaces, and a neighbourhood ice cream truck man who rolled the fattest blunts with the homies after selling cold treats to the kids. Unlike gated communities, on our block, in every season except winter, our streets were flooded with people 24/7. We lived in the kind of hood where everyone was outside.

On the block, family wasn't about blood. Family was the people you grew up with and who looked out for you. In human years I was seven; in block years I was 21. Around Block 13, based on our experiences—what we see, hear, and experience first-hand in these streets—we were seen as being at least double our age if not more. What made things worse was that as Black youth, in the eyes of the teachers and law enforcement, we were seen as less innocent and were treated more like adults than our white counterparts. They protected us children less and punished us more, simply for existing with our different skin colour. In their eyes, we were guilty before innocent, dangerous before friendly, and criminal before human.

The streets impacted our mental health and it was hard to tell how much of our childhood innocence we had left. We children felt the heaviness of the world on our shoulders instead of the weightless freedom of play.

One day in June, just days after school had let out for the summer, I was sitting on my porch in the middle of the red brick housing complex, the sunlight beaming through the broken streetlights above my head. This was my observation booth to watch the block—who came in and who came out. Every day there were moments of happiness and laughter. Kids racing around the block doing wheelies on their bikes, roller skating up and down the sidewalk with no breaks, youth riding two feet tall mini motorcycles with no registration, double dutchin' and drawing hopscotch in the middle of the street, soccer tournaments, BBQs at the community centre, block parties, Cee-lo hustlers cracking jokes and freestyling or storytelling on the corner, shooting basketballs on rims with no net, arguments in the ball court over a missed foul call, and the slap of Dominoes loud enough to break the wooden table or neighbourhood electrical greenbox. To top it all off was the melanin-rich music blaring so loud that we thought it was a competition to see who could make the speaker explode the fastest. With R&B, motown, reggae, dancehall, and a huge amount of hip hop and rap music, the genres were always on point. Every track the older heads played always felt like a certified banger.

"Curtis, come eat! I gotta go!" my mom screamed out the kitchen window.

It was rare to eat at the same time as my parents as it seemed they were always at work or on their way somewhere. My parents were normally working three plus jobs, day and night shifts. They worked for something we called the Agency. I couldn't keep track of all the places they worked but I knew it was a factory job of some sort, sometimes in cities outside of Toronto, costing them three to four hours, roundtrip. I wished eating dinner with my family was a daily event but around my hood these moments were more like annual events, once a month or once a week if you were lucky. Usually, dinner was just me and my older brothers.

We were first generation Canadians. My parents had immigrated from Guyana in the late 1980s. In search of a new life and a fresh start for us kids, they didn't arrive empty-handed. They came with fried plantain, curry chicken, roti and dhal puri, cassava, eddoes, cook up rice, peas and rice, sugar cane, pepper pot, bake and saltfish, Caribbean black cake, bora, chow mein, sorrel drink, every tropical fruit and vegetable you could think of, and spicy achar and pepper sauce which, depending on the day, was the equivalent of eating lava. This was our first taste of home before we could find the money to visit.

From my bedroom window, I watched as my mom hobbled to

catch the 69 or 135 bus that I swear comes once every 24 hours. The rain began to sprinkle, about to go full Noah's Ark, as I stared at her standing in the distance at a bus shelter with no roof and observed the drug dealer on the corner in the parking lot. Two individuals, two different paths, opposite hustles but both with the same goal of putting food on the table. Society sees these two as completely different but from what I saw as a kid, they were two sides of the same coin—rain or shine, they wanted to provide for the family and keep the lights on. They were both just down the street from me, but on an emotional level, they felt light-years away.

The majority of people in my neighbourhood were making an honest living doing whatever jobs they needed to do to make ends meet. We weren't lazy and weren't all on government assistance as falsely depicted on the news. We were society's true hustlers. Our parents, like many, were busy juggling a million jobs and did their best to raise us. But because their time was limited, I spent more time in the streets. Tallying up the hours, my parents did not raise me on their own, the streets were my co-parent. I remember the corner that embraced me. The concrete where we laughed, cried, hustled, and where the OGs poured some out for the ones we lost.

Outside in the streets, the older heads gave me three guidelines that became my M.O. (modus operandi) when arriving in any new hood or environment: 1) observe to find out who's who and what's what, 2) respect is earned, not given, and 3) be aware of your surroundings. We had to know who was on the board and where all the pieces were because people were making moves on the daily and we needed to know how to manoeuvre on the block. We had to play a couple moves ahead of the game so we didn't get stuck as a pawn or get into the middle of any situation that went south. This was crucial so we kept everything that was ours and didn't get punked off by people taking our stuff because we didn't see it coming.

In the midst of it all there were realities we didn't quite understand until we were older and had the words for it. The jobs might not call us back when they see the postal code on our resume and cover letter. Public transit fees will keep increasing while the quality of service decreases on our side of the city. Hoods in the city got the worst bus service, with overcrowded buses and longer wait times than the wealthier communities. The banks and payday loan businesses prey on our lack of financial understanding. Convenience stores quadruple their prices for things we have to buy because they know the grocery store is marathons away from our block. If we needed something, we really had to go on a mission to get it. This was our hood. This was our norm—isolation. Not much would change over the years other than the arrival of new families who were forced to move out of their hoods and relocate to ours.

The city had a practice of pushing poor, Black, and brown families out of their own neighbourhoods, demolishing the community fabric, and then replacing the block with wealthy—mostly white—people and corporations who almost always didn't look like us or come from the same block. The majority of families were forced to relocate to public housing hoods across the city and had limited choices of where they could go. Then they would keep only a tiny percentage of us in the newly renovated neighbourhood. These "decision makers" who worked for the city moved like snakes. They never told us straight to our face what they were up to, they just put a "fancy" urban renewal label on it and called it gentrification. But we called it how we saw it. Gentrification wasn't new. It was historical and it was happening across the country and south of our border.

When random businesses like an expensive coffee shop or restaurant magically appeared in your hood that no one—not a single soul—in your community vibes or connects with, you knew those developers walking through your block were cooking something up. They often gave us a sports facility and an art installation as a thank you, so I guess that's a "fair" trade. We were segregated by race and income all across Toronto and Canada, and to figure out what was actually happening then was as simple as a Google search.

I often wondered if our neighbourhoods were underfunded and not well-maintained to make sure gentrification was the government's only pitch for improving the community. At that moment, we knew these were Costco-sized pills we had to swallow. We had to learn from the beautiful words of scholar, revolutionary, rapper, and activist, Tupac Shakur—son to Afeni Shakur, a former Black Panther Party member—to see what was really going on: "If you let a person talk long enough, you'll hear their true intentions. Listen twice, speak once."

Before the global craze of social media mobile apps, the worldwide use of smartphones, and the 24 hours of daily screen time, we were the kids who played outside. We didn't know we were low-income until we went to elementary school and heard the way the teachers talked about our neighbourhood in relation to their gated communities in the suburbs. We didn't have much, but we were proud of being from the block. If we didn't have opportunities, we created our own.

CITY OF TORONTO BUDGET AND FUNDING

YEAR	EMPLOYMENT	SCHOOL OPERATIONS	POLICE
2003	$10.3 million	$530 million	$669 million
2004	10.5 "	460 "	707 "
2005	10.7 "	430 "	753 "
2006	11.1 "	430 "	799 "
2007	11.9 "	410 "	829 "

Dr. Alex

Age ten: My neighbourhood homie Alex was 12 years old when he received his PhD. This wasn't any ol' university degree. He didn't go to school for decades listening to talking heads in lecture halls or go into $100,000+ worth of debt to get this far. He received this PhD from the block. This stamp of approval on his life was for the combination of raw talent and skills he developed in the streets where he worked as an entrepreneur and inventor. One day in July 2003, just weeks before going back to school, he attempted his most ambitious project yet. He set out to build his own unique motorcycle. Our block was a food desert and he wanted to make grocery trips faster. In government housing projects, with limited resources, programs, and opportunities, this was seen as a courageous mission. But not to Alex. He would do anything, by any means, to help his family and community.

"Crossover. Step-back jumper! Kobe!"

"Glass! You can't guard me. Take a seat. That's game! Who got next?"

The neighbourhood ball court, 52, was crowded every weekend, all day, and every evening. Not much else to do to pass the time other than trying to play ball like Jordan, Black Mamba, or Vince Carter. Full court 5 vs. 5 with the young ones from Southside to North in the metal cage covered with green bars as fences. The bleachers were crowded with at least 20 kids waiting to see who got to play next. And as always, the best person on the court always had the freshest Kobes or Jordans on their feet. They were so nice that if you left them unattended, they would be scooped up and flipped for cash in a second.

I was sitting on the edge of my seat in the front row, ready to watch the next game. The summer sky was ocean blue with the sun at its highest point and the smooth breeze blowing, just a few weeks away from the Caribana heat. The game was poetry in motion—rhythmic dribbling vibrating the ground, shoes squeaking, kids running so fast it felt like an earthquake. The pickup runs were always life or death serious but the crowd almost always eventually collapsed with laughter as someone got dunked on, dropped by a crossover, or roasted in a freestyle battle in the bleachers.

"Play D, bro! This is not football, stop hugging me."

I glanced at the back of the bleachers, and there was Alex. He was daydreaming, happiness in public. This is what he looked like when he had a problem on his mind. He wouldn't give it a break until he solved it.

Alex was a product of the 1990s. He was a 90s baby from the southside of our block. His swag was inspired by JAY-Z and the hip hop duo Kris Kross—he wore a Toronto Raptors Vince Carter jersey backwards and baggy Rocawear jeans circa 2003 that could easily fit his older brother. The long white tee underneath and his all-white Nike Air Force 1s made it the full package. To top it off, he always had the freshest braid up—looking like Allen Iverson. This was the 90s baby swag. He was like many of us on the block, creating opportunities out of nothing. Sometimes kids would pick on him because his intelligence was intimidating, but his swagger was mad cool and got him a hall pass when needed. Alex used to be a drug runner—dropping drugs at spots infrequently for quick cash—but was never interested in being a curb server. Curb servers were runners who graduated. They used their skills to run a business 24/7/365.

Alex was more interested in inventing and repairing things. If there was a broken door, busted lock, broken scooter—whatever it was, he would fix it. Problems motivated him to work smart and hard to find a solution. He learned these skills from his mom, dad, and older brother—all working-class people who immigrated from Jamaica. They all had hidden creative talents buried deep within them. From his family, he learned to be a bike and car mechanic, a standard plumber and house maintenance expert, a laundry and lawn-cutter pro. In his spare time, he developed entrepreneurial skills from the corner servers, all while keeping up with his Grade 6 homework. He was a learner by circumstance. He knew it was cheaper to fix it yourself than pay for help with money you didn't have.

From the back of the bleachers, he rose suddenly. Jumping down from the grass hill bleachers, he started to run up the stairs and around the vacant recreation centre. I stood up, ran up to the south end of the court to the top of the hill and looked into the school field from behind the caged fence. My eyes were scrambling. I was having trouble locating him in the distance. Squinting my eyes, I finally spotted him sprinting across the Warden Avenue School field, towards Southside. Leyton Avenue. His home.

His body was getting smaller and smaller in the distance. In his hand, he was carrying something I couldn't quite identify. Curious to see, I followed his lead. I ran down the hill, up the stairs, and around the recreation centre.

Sprinting across the field, I started a domino effect. I knew the whole squad would follow my lead.

"All the mandem! Pull up!"

"Bet!"

We had limited access to grocery stores and healthy food options as the No Frills and Price Chopper were an hour's walk away, or 90 minutes if you walked cool. If you did not have bus fare, a bike, or other means of commuting, you were forced to walk. Over the years, Alex became sick and tired of accepting this reality. Living in isolation, locked in by the forest that surrounds our hood, Alex always planned to find a solution one day. The bikes shared around the hood were always in use by someone doing errands so if you needed it and it wasn't available, you'd have to take transit. But if you only had enough money for food, you couldn't afford transit. The only option left was to walk it out. This is where Alex came in. We knew grandmas, moms, and pops were not going to bike groceries home, so he created a solution that allowed the kids to do it for them.

I arrived in his backyard before my other homies, though I felt as if I'd left my lungs at the ball court. My knees were screaming at me. My toes were mad crushed. My head on a swivel, like the head of a city pigeon, I looked around at the utter chaos of his backyard, trying to distract myself from my (now) see-through white tee as I attempted to catch my breath. On the northside fence: dozens of bike tires and bike tubes. Southside: toaster ovens, blenders, and lawn mower parts. In the middle of the patched-up grass were dozens of bike frames, many of which were broken. Knowing Alex and his resourcefulness, I could sense the five-finger discount applied to at least some of the stuff. Some stuff he got from garbage bins, like old appliances neighbours didn't use. His process was simple. Define the problem, brainstorm solutions, build a model, test it, and then improve it until the solution is successful. "I'll stop when I'm done" was his motto. I was lucky enough to see Alex's talents in action as he worked through the final stages of testing his motorcycle prototype with our squad as his audience.

"Ahhhhhhhhh! He's going to bless the block with a Kawasaki, fam!"

"One eighty in a ninety zone, juss now!"

"This some Einstein shit, homie!"

Usually, Alex worked in quiet with his older brother but sometimes, when he wanted time away from his projects, he came to play with us. Right in front of our eyes, Alex built a bike from scratch, attaching a Dollarama cooling fan to control the engine temperature and topping it off with an engine cover so it wouldn't burn your inner legs as you ride. With mad confidence, he was ready for people to put respect on his name. Especially those teachers who said we block kids had no skills or talents. The truth was, we were born with more than enough creativity; it was the school system that attempted to kill it and bury it deep within us. Alex helped us realize that we were all gold mines, each of us. Watching him made a lot of us believe anything was possible.

"No yute on the block is missioning an hour deep to get food again. On my name."

Alex didn't have a fear of failure. He would work for months on dozens and dozens of prototypes, never quitting until he figured it out. Using every loss as a lesson, he made a better decision on his next steps each time he was up to bat. After testing several models, improving and refining them, like magic, Alex was able to create the first motor bicycle I'd ever seen in my life, years before they were popularized in the city. I was ten years old and totally amazed.

Pulling the engine rope, as one would pull the gas-powered lawn mower to start, the motorcycle was birthed. Summer '03 was officially legendary.

"My DAWGGGGGGGGGG! Super Saiyan typa shit!"

One by one, everyone ran up to Alex, slapping palms and sliding them to closed fists. The daps from the entire crew was the block hug, the only type of hug you got from the homies. This was the moment he received his street PhD. The moment where he felt brilliant. Something he'd never felt in school, only on the block. He wasn't some dead white engineer or scientist from a black and white photo. He was here in the flesh. Turning his invention into a business, Alex and his older brother eventually upgraded a limited supply of bikes in our community to make them gas-powered. Making money to help out at home was always a mark of honour and respect in the hood. Respect was not given, it was earned.

Alex was only 12 and he was our street scientist and hood philosopher. He never spoke empty words or brought us religion. What he did bring was a wealth of knowledge and tools for application. To him, the street corner was a place for business, innovation, and creativity. Life rewarded us for making connections and applying it to the real world. School rewarded us for memorizing information only to regurgitate it, again and again. In the world outside of school, on the block, we didn't think and process things in a straight line, one subject at a time. For us, everything was nonlinear, not like school, which had a tendency to celebrate linear thinking as it punished creativity. This process wasn't as relevant or transferable to a world that doesn't operate in a straight line. That day, I'd finally understood what Tupac meant by "the rose that grew from concrete;" someone who made something of themselves despite their circumstances. With Alex's invention, I experienced for the first—but not last—time what roses in the concrete jungle felt and looked like. It started off as a deep desire to build the motorcycle he couldn't afford as a child, and it turned into his own business, providing a solution to the problem of food deserts that plagued Toronto's public housing hoods like ours.

Alex was addressing a need. Starting his shop with the help of his older brother, just a freshman in high school, their simple invention became a community service that used limited supplies to help others share in the joy of having their very own motor bicycle. At that moment, many of us watched in awe and without a clue as to how to explain what he did. The thinking process of many of us on the block had been to use our creativity and resourcefulness to survive in a world that gave us limited resources. The major difference with Alex was his ability to channel his creativity into invention and entrepreneurship. With some further discussion over the years, I saw myself as able to learn and do what Alex did by shadowing him while he worked. Seeing his craft in action gave the block inspiration and motivated me personally to start my own local bike shop a year later.

Alex wasn't just an engineer. He was an engineer with a soul. An engineer with a soul is what the world refers to as a designer. An individual whose level of care for our community gave him a desire to create meaningful solutions using his own innovative designs. What started off as a cool experiment became the launch of a motor bicycle shop where Alex and his brother flipped bikes for cash, meeting the community's demand.

Around Alex, I felt like I could try new things and fail because he never judged us and he encouraged every kid on the block to keep trying until we got it. Between Alex and corner boys selling rocks, I felt like I had a purpose and that I was important to the block. When the block boys dap me up or big us up, sometimes that's the only affirmation, the only love, we get outside of our own home.

As humans, we flock towards places that make us feel brilliant. Unfortunately, sometimes we couldn't find that place in school or at home. With parents working a million jobs to survive and pay the bills and with families broken apart or loved ones stolen from us, I, like many others, found my place on the corner with whoever was available to us, like Dr. Alex and the curb servers.

Alex's passion for inventing things made him a street legend. To design what he did, going through all the necessary steps to come up with a solution to the problem, he taught us how to not take no for an answer. In the eyes of the world, the process that Alex used to design solutions was known as the **Engineering Design Process**.

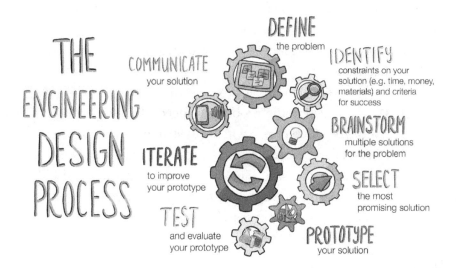

THE ENGINEERING DESIGN PROCESS

COMMUNICATE your solution

DEFINE the problem

IDENTIFY constraints on your solution (e.g. time, money, materials) and criteria for success

BRAINSTORM multiple solutions for the problem

ITERATE to improve your prototype

SELECT the most promising solution

TEST and evaluate your prototype

PROTOTYPE your solution

The Engineering Design Process is a series of steps an engineer takes to define the problem and create a solution. This process is focused on building, designing, prototyping, testing, and improving a product or process until it solves the defined problem. Growing up, we just called this survival—turning nothing into something—aka the block trademark.

We weren't old enough or educated enough to articulate how he did what he did. Later though, we understood Alex's natural process of solving problems with the mind of an engineer and a love for the block. Everything he designed was to make the hood better and give others opportunities to try something new. At the time, we did not know that the process Alex used was also used to create things like airplanes, robotics equipment, space craft, buildings and bridges, medical devices, water treatment and waste management centres, computers and networks, microprocessors, operating systems, home appliances, the Internet, food and drinks, electronics, metalwork, mobile apps, application software, earth mineral extraction machines, and even lawn care appliances like the motorized lawn mower Alex used.

He brought family and friends to his backyard to speak about his product from start to finish, talking about its purpose and its ability to meet the community's needs. Those who were interested could get Alex and his brother to help them build their own motorcycle for a small fee (payment for labour and parts).

Alex was a creative genius. If I were to break it down step-by-step, this is what he did:

1. **Define** – Define the problem or need: The neighbourhood was a food desert with a 60–90 minute walk to the closest grocery store. Alex wanted to decrease transportation time and save money by finding alternatives to travel instead of paying a fare to use public transit.
2. **Identify** – Do your research: Gain knowledge and insights into target users and pre-existing solutions.

Users Walking: 60–90 minute walk to grocery store (primary option)

Biking: Borrowing bikes from neighbours (limited number and sizes available in neighbourhood; some bikes too small for the older youth/adults to use) (secondary option)

Transit: 60+ minute wait for the bus; transit fee expensive for families working an unlivable wage (third option)

Car Share: Neighbours carpooling to do grocery trips for multiple families (fourth option; not as common as people who drove were usually at work)

Looking at the options, Alex needed to create a transportation option that was affordable/low cost and gets the community to the grocery store faster than just walking/biking (especially given kids bikes have fixed gears).

3. **Brainstorm** – Brainstorm multiple ideas for solutions: One option was to buy bikes with higher speeds with the money we could make selling drugs, cutting grass, shovelling sidewalks in the winter, or stealing bikes or dollar store items to flip for cash. Alex did not want anyone to get in trouble with the law so he had the idea to build his own motor bicycle and start his own business.

4. **Select** – Choose the most promising solution: Build a personalized motor bicycle by repurposing existing equipment he could find in the community.

5. **Prototype** – Build a prototype: Alex built the bike from scratch using broken/damaged bike parts and other electronics gathered from garbage bins, including toaster ovens, blenders, microwaves, and lawn mower engines. He built a sample engine to see if it would start.

6. **Test** – Test and evaluate prototype: Learn what works and doesn't work then fix it to make a better end product. Alex worked on bikes for at least four months to consistently test and evaluate motor bicycles from start to finish using dozens and dozens of prototypes. Using feedback from the OGs on the block he continued to refine the engine until it worked without shutting off or stalling.

7. **Iterate** – Make changes to improve prototypes and repeat the entire engineering process until it meets the needs of people who will use it: To make the motor bicycle ridable, Alex replaced plastic zip ties with metal ones and attached a cooling fan to control the engine temperature and an engine cover to prevent riders legs from burning.

8. **Communicate** – Present the final product and start making sales.

To the school system, he was just Alex. But to us he was Dr. Alex. His impact and legacy made the hood history books, not the school HIStory books that were filled with misinformation and skewed narratives as told by the "winners" (aka colonial powers).

At just 12 years old, Dr. Alex's transferable skills in engineering, mathematics, entrepreneurship, and leadership proved how creativity and resourcefulness can grow from the broken pavement. Alex was the type to ask questions, imagine possible solutions, and plan out designs to experiment with. He never stopped questioning and never stopped working on the problem until he found a solution. To him, the questions were more important than the answers.

Early on, through our public education system, those around me were misled to believe that because of our skin colour and postal code we did not have much value to offer the world. But in reality, we were skilled in many areas, possessing raw talent and genius. The major issue was limited platforms to showcase it.

Yet, all the while, teachers had continued to stay ignorant about how our hoods functioned. They were the ones unwilling to learn and go the extra mile. In many cases, many of them never stepped foot in the neighbourhood where they taught, even if it was ten steps across the street.

We often wondered how this type of teacher was allowed in front of us kids. They would teach from a place of ignorance and miseducation that made public school another kind of prison. This was the biggest injustice millions of Black, brown, and poor kids had to deal with every day. In the city of Toronto and across the country, from grade school to high school, we were disproportionately streamed into courses below our ability, received less educational support from teachers and were told by guidance counsellors that university and academic courses were not for us, and were suspended and expelled at higher rates than white students. Day to day, existing and breathing felt like a crime.

Teachers and principals seemed more focused on securing the bag, getting paid, and sending us to the office just for asking a question than creating a safe environment for us to learn. They had the audacity to tell me I should smile more, but ain't nothing to smile about. I loved to learn and I liked education, just not school. To me school and education were not synonymous.

When I was in grade school, I would peep out the backyard window to stare at the stars twinkling above the Warden Woods forest that hugged the block. From time to time, around 4:00 a.m., after a washroom break, I would see a few black-on-black vans tip toe up the street with a full roster of raid-ready cops. Unmarked cargo vans. Twenty cops deep. All black everything. War ready and equipped with AK-47 looking straps. Drawn and loaded. I saw this before and always prayed for the family—especially for the kids—whose door was about to fly off the hinges. With the row of houses blocking my view, the cops were too far away for me to pinpoint which house they were about to storm into. Warrant or not, they would still bulldoze your door and draw guns on little children.

If the police were caught participating in criminal activity or committing murder, they would almost always beat the case or get suspended with full pay. I didn't understand how they rarely got punished for their crimes until I was older. Since the cops wrote the police reports and did the paperwork for all incidents of criminal activity, even if they were caught, they could find a loophole to cover their tracks and alter the paperwork or evidence. This is happening in the present day in my city and worldwide, but it has been a typical part of policing since its origins. Policing was a different kind of monster. And school sadly was no different. In many ways, they were arms of the same monster.

We deserve better from the city. We deserve more than the basketball courts and street murals the city tries to give us year after year. More than shady police and neglectful schools. We wanted and needed more opportunities.

Toronto to Vancouver

Location: *Maple Creek, Saskatchewan*
(Alberta–Saskatchewan border)
July 5, 2017, 3:30 a.m.: *Westbound to Vancouver,*
British Columbia

I never really left the four-city block of my neighbourhood until I was 17. And now, at 24, I was in the middle of the province of Saskatchewan, driving in the westbound lane of the Trans-Canada Highway headed towards Vancouver, British Columbia, 3074 km from my neighbourhood of Block 13. I was cruising in a Ford Expedition seven-seater SUV. In the passenger seat, snoring himself to sleep, was my friend Addisiane, and fast asleep in the backseat, snuggled under a mountain of Walmart blankets and pillows we had by the dozen, were Jarrett and Cameron, their heads nuzzled into the crevices of the car doors. This was my Ride for Promise support van team. They would help me cycle across Canada.

Observing the transport and pickup trucks zooming by me in the darkness and the smell of burnt rubber invading my nostrils, I struggled to keep my eyelids open as we drove through the endless flatlands of the Prairies. The Prairies are the grassland, plains, and lowlands of the southern regions of the provinces of Manitoba, Saskatchewan, and

Alberta. The one thing they had in common was that they were mad flat with lots of farmland and barely any people or trees, just a lot of John Deere tractors and machinery used for mowing and seeding the farmland, and Canadian flags rippling in the wind at every house we saw. The people I did see looked at me like they'd never seen a Black person in their life. Some places looked deserted, like the typical scary movies where the only Black person in the film dies first. This was the exact opposite of what I saw growing up in the city.

Being from Scarborough, I was accustomed to a million down-town condo buildings, overcrowded transit buses, and thick forests around the outskirts. Driving through the Prairies, I felt like I was physically not moving or making any progress. For thousands and thousands of kilometres all around us, it all looked the same. I once heard that Saskatchewan is one of the flattest places in the world, but to me, it was the flattest place on the planet. In grade school, we learned that the Prairies are a major source of wheat, petroleum, nat-ural gas, agriculture, and livestock, and that they have football-sized fields full of bundles and bundles of haystacks. Reading about the Prairies was one thing, but being out here in real life was eye-opening for a kid like me who grew up only knowing the streets and concrete jungle of Toronto.

We were one week from the start of the Ride for Promise. Before cycling across the country, we first had to travel to the west coast from Toronto. We were driving 4400 kilometres in three days to reach Van-couver. We weren't planning on making many stops and had every-thing we needed in the van or in the enclosed cargo trailer attached to our van. In the trailer, we had three bikes, all of our food and water for the summer, camping supplies, tents, portable gas-powered BBQs, books, 50 pounds of Bulk Barn candy, basketball shoes and sports equipment, and the most important thing, our hammocks. We would stay in Vancouver a few days to get used to the time difference, as Van-couver is three hours behind Toronto. But this also gave us an excuse to see the mountains that surround the entire city. I would start biking from Vancouver to Halifax on July 10, spending the rest of the summer riding from the Pacific Ocean to the Atlantic Ocean, so I had a few days to chill and load up on food before the ride officially started.

My support team had two main objectives to help me cycle across Canada successfully. First, we had to enjoy the trip like a vacation, visiting the mountains, oceans, and national park lakes that we had only ever seen in the movies and on social media. Second, they had to make sure I was well fed, hydrated, and didn't fall off a cliff. Basically, they were there to help me make it across Canada in one piece. To make that possible, Addisiane had to cycle with me every day, coast to coast, to keep me company as we cycled into every city stop. Jarrett was our team videographer. He was there to take photos and videos of the entire journey. Support van drivers are key to the success of a ride, and Cameron was our main driver for one month, from Vancouver to Toronto. The support van had to drive ahead of us as we cycled to meet us at safety checkpoints. The drivers would check in with us by phone or text throughout the day, and they scheduled roadside water and food pickups. If we got lost, the driver would give guidance on where to go. When we arrived in Toronto, my high school homies Bligh and Trey would take over for Cameron, driving from Toronto to Halifax. This was the dream team.

As I drove into the darkness on these country roads, I had one hour until I had to wake the team up to see the sunrise. We were sleeping in shifts, three hour blocks where two people stayed awake and two people slept. Addisiane missed his morning shift because he'd been asleep for the past two hours. With my right hand, I reached over to the dash and put on a random radio station playing country music. I was cool with it, as the vibe matched the country roads that were passing right before my eyes, so I turned up the volume midway to keep my eyes alert and open. I had too much time to kill being alone and my mind started racing as I reflected on everything that had happened to bring us to this current moment.

Thousands of people throughout history have cycled across Canada. The two most common reasons: 1) to check it off their bucket list and 2) to raise money and awareness for cancer research. These were amazing initiatives. Our ride across Canada was different because it was focused on challenging systemic racism in Canada. We were raising funds for afterschool programs in low-income communities across Toronto. I chose to use the ride as a vehicle for awareness and to raise money for Urban Promise Toronto, an organization that hosts afterschool programs in largely Black communities. At the time, they had programs in Rexdale, the neighbourhoods surrounding Jane and Finch, and my neighbourhood, Block 13, in Scarborough.

It took me a whole year to gather the people I needed to make Ride for Promise possible. I sent 500 emails, made 250 phone calls, had 100 in-person meetings, trained for 328 hours, and cycled 9184 km. I started off with a five-kilometre ride in Scarborough and worked my way up to the ten-kilometre ride to downtown Toronto. I almost physically died on the corner of Nathan Phillips Square as my heart was exploding out of my ears. Eventually, I cycled 215 km in one day, from Markham to Muskoka, to get road ready.

I didn't reach out to just anyone. I brainstormed the type of person I needed first and then did hundreds of searches on Google, Twitter, Instagram, and LinkedIn until I found the people I was looking for. I Googled how to send professional emails instead of the "Yo" that start all my emails. I knew that my connections on the block wouldn't be enough to make it happen so I built relationships and got to know people in different industries and different fields. And I stayed confident in my vision from day one. The people that helped out also caught the vision and felt like they were part of something bigger than themselves.

In my community outreach campaigns, I reached out online to people I thought could help fund the Ride for Promise. There were over 850 emails, text messages, and phone calls, but in the end, all I needed was the 16 people who donated their money and time to help us fund the ride. The crazy part was that the business sponsorships and individual donations all came through only one month before the ride started. I felt like I was daydreaming.

Of all the people we reached out to across Canada, my success rate was only 1.88%—but it was all I needed. With these wins, we were able to rent an SUV for the entire summer, plus a trailer that hooked onto the hitch of the SUV to carry all our equipment and supplies. Our support van team donated their time, sacrificing their summer, and my cycling coaches Neil (a former cross-Canada cyclist) and his son Cameron volunteered to get me physically and mentally ready to ride across Canada. People hooked us up with money for gas, bike equipment, food, and supplies, and to top it off, film director and producer Sherien Barsoum joined our team.

Sherien had heard about Ride for Promise and wanted to document the ride across Canada and pitch the film at the Hot Docs Short Film festival. Out of hundreds of applicants, we were awarded first place and received $30,000 from BravoFACT to film the ride. Sherien was a director and producer for numerous documentaries screened all over the world. Without her, we wouldn't have had the chance to document whether we made it across the country or died trying.

Our plan was simple: cycle coast to coast, bike 100 to 215 km every day for the entire summer. Along the way, we would stop in 30 different cities and stay overnight with families who were kind enough to welcome us into their homes. These families would make us meals, give us a warm place to sleep and food for the road, and they would also organize speaking events in their backyards, community centres, churches, and parking lots, giving me the chance to speak to audiences about why we were riding in the first place.

Through our donors and charitable organizations like Urban Promise, we had a list of people who would welcome us each day in each city. In total, I lead a 60-person team, with my support van team, overnight hosts, and event organizers in each city. I had a stacked resume not by choice but by circumstance. I was the founder, CEO, manager, cyclist, and speaker for Ride for Promise, and the leading figure in the documentary, videos, and photos. It wasn't easy to have a million roles, but it was what I needed to do to get things started. This was only the beginning of Ride for Promise, and I was sleep deprived before the ride even started.

Plan A was to cycle across Canada. I didn't have a plan B. In my mind a plan B would distract from plan A. Ever since I was a kid, whatever I said I was going to do, I did it. There was no other option. I didn't announce publicly I was cycling across Canada until two weeks before it started. I learned to never announce your moves because life is like chess. I needed to move with my feet rather than my mouth. I had a plan. A step-by-step list written down from start to finish. In the end, everything happened exactly as I envisioned it. The only thing left was for me to finish the bike ride across Canada.

After three hours of driving in darkness, in a split second, an epic orange haze splashed across the black sky from east to west. For a moment, I felt like I was watching the original Lion King movie when Rafiki stood on Pride Rock and held Simba up to the sky so all the animals could see Mufasa's son. One thing I appreciated about the flatland was that you can see the sun from beginning to end without any buildings or the thousands of condos blocking it. As the sunlight beamed through the windows on the passenger side, the team slowly woke up, just in time to catch the sunrise over the CN rail tracks cutting through the farmland. Using my left hand, I flicked the handles sticking out from behind the steering wheel to signal right. Going from a cruise to a stop, I parked on the shoulder of the Trans-Canada Highway. Spraying my windshield washer fluid ten more times, I wiped off the thousand bugs that were splattered on it. I took the keys out of the ignition and just chilled until they got the memo that it was time to wake up.

We were almost 3000 km from Toronto with only 1000 km left until we arrived in Vancouver. My eyelids started to quiver so I knew I had to knock out as soon as I could after catching the views. Within seconds, my mind started to wander and my stomach started to drop as I wrestled with questions I couldn't answer. *How come I haven't seen cops since leaving southern Ontario?*

Where I grew up, cops swarmed our neighbourhood and harassed us 24/7/365. They racially profiled us, toyed with us psychologically to force us to give them our information, beat us up in alleyways, and performed no-knock police raids without warrants. I was accustomed to seeing them plant drugs on my homies. The message is clear: it's a crime to be poor and Black. From what I could see, people who live in the suburbs or the country or own lots of real estate and land don't have these kinds of interactions with the police. We tried to record our interactions with police, but when it comes to getting away with crime, murder, assault, harassment, money laundering, corruption, and planting drugs on innocent people, the police always win. They always get fat pensions. We rarely see justice.

Those of us in the hood may be on the same planet as the cops, but we live in two completely different worlds. Canada is not glorious and free for everyone. We felt both free and not free, living in public housing. There was a reason my heart started racing and the rhythm of my breathing skyrocketed when I saw cops patrolling. Looking back at my life, I see that my feelings about and interactions with cops could be traced back to when the cops raided my house when I was a kid. Bootleg warrant. No knock. No announcement. Same stuff, different day.

Knock Knock, Who's There?

> *Please try to remember that what they believe, as well as what they do and cause you to endure does not testify to your inferiority but to their inhumanity. I can't believe what you say, because I see what you do.*
>
> —James Baldwin

Age nine: In almost every crime movie there is a key scene where undercover police stake out a trap house. In the middle of the night, cops break a door down and charge in with full force. "Freeze! Don't move!" The first person immediately starts running, creating a domino effect. Everyone follows suit in an attempt to run to freedom. Out the back door, one person can be seen getting away. Suddenly, they're tackled by the SWAT team through the back alley. Everyone gets handcuffed. The cops seize all the drugs or guns. The cops drive back to the station, and the detained are thrown in jail. Then a celebration over donuts and drinks. The End.

Whenever I see that scene, I always think it's a joke. As a Black, Indigenous, or brown person in the projects, when the cops say *freeze* you morph into the best freeze tag statue you can just to stay alive. If you run—or move an inch in even the least threatening way—you risk being shot to death or beaten; something way worse than getting tackled. Gun-drawing, trigger-happy cops were the norm in our city, on these blocks—especially during a police raid.

Usually, the cops came in groups at night to harass, card, and yell at us kids, letting us know that to them we were criminals. Some got cocky enough to call us the n-word. If you talked back, they'd be sure to toss you to the ground. If you resisted their harassment, they'd stomp on you. Our interactions were complicated.

I will never forget the day the police broke down my front door with a "search warrant." It was a Sunday. I was nine years old.

Sundays were monumental for our block. During the summer, the block was usually flooded with kids. We played in the field or rode our bikes in the early hours as some parents came back from their night shifts and the next crew left to clock-in for the morning shifts. No days off—straight hustle. Parents were sleeping during the day after the night shift, preparing to go to church or mosque, or just chilling on front porches watching the addicts look for food from the curb servers—that's when you know their cheques came in. School was closed, or as my boy Dr. Alex would say, "The prison is under renovation." The security guards and prison governor had gone home. Summer was our freedom.

We lived in typical Toronto public housing. One long rectangular building split into 14 two-storey housing units. We were squished into the end unit in a three-bedroom closest to the main strip, called Cataraqui Crescent—I could basically hear my neighbours breathe. My mom had a room that she shared with my dad whenever he was home and not working. The second room was for my older brother. My other brother and I shared the best room of the house: the red bunkbed room. My brother got the bottom and I got the top of the castle—the throne. Our room was baby blue, and our windows looked out over two dozen backyards. We could even see the basketball court across the street. We were literally the centre of the block, at the heart of the strip where most things went down. Same shit, different day.

One day in July, just a couple weeks after school let out for the summer, my mom was heading into the kitchen to make ginger tea, having just arrived home from the late shift. I was asleep upstairs. My older brothers were at a friend's house that night for a sleepover. I hadn't wanted to go; staying home was my motive. They entered just before sunrise. No "good morning," no happy "God is good" Sunday. In the movies they come at night, but here they were in the bright sunshine of the early morning. The front door burst open, blowing off the hinges and denting the wall behind it. A crew of at least ten police flooded the house, commencing a flurry of screams of worry and confusion that echoed up the walls, waking me.

"Mom?"

Still drowsy and not fully present, my first instinct was to check on my mom. Opening my eyes and sitting up, I heard the sound of heavy military boots vibrating the house. There were numerous bodies in the house within seconds.

"Police!"

I was awake now. I was no longer dreaming. I quickly surmised that this was not TV; it was actually happening. This was real life. My eyes were popping out of my skull as I heard boots moving at hyper speed below me, running from the front door through our hallway to the backdoor. Another set of feet ran from the backdoor to our kitchen and the basement. Eventually they made their way towards me, and they were coming quickly, as if it were a race. Tossing my blanket to the ground, I jumped off the top bunk and onto the frosty floor beneath me. The moment I stood up, planting my feet in the centre of the room, staring at the door like a deer caught in headlights, the door flew open.

The cop standing in the doorway of my bedroom quickly reached for his gun. I felt in control of my body, but my insides were screaming for help. I was stuck—stuck in quicksand in the middle of the room. I forgot how to breathe. Staring dead in the eye of this stone cold Steve Austin look-alike, I wondered if he was in the wrong profession. The cop and I had a stare down. My curiosity and confusion did not match his gaze. I had seen this look before.

He was startled way before he saw me, but it just got worse as we stood there. I saw the look in his eyes and wished I didn't recognize it. It was a look that seemed to justify being scared of me. I was just a kid, but to him, I was a criminal.

When the number of shootings in the neighbourhood started feeling higher than average, everyone knew summer had arrived. The temperature of the streets followed the trend of the weather. When it was hot and humid it was *hot and humid*. So, when he reached for the gun, I could hear the gunshots in my head so audibly that it felt as if my ear drums were going to pop. I could hear the emptying of clips and the bouncing shell cases skipping like rocks across the broken pavement. My hands were sticky and salty. I have never felt so extremely hot and extremely cold at the same time. My mouth was dry. I swallowed hard. Without knowing it, I was holding my breath. One moment you could be alive, just trying to be a kid, and the next you could be on a T-shirt. I wish I'd had the words back then to explain my experience, but I had been conditioned to believe that *boys don't cry*. I wanted to cry, but my heart was stone. I felt like someone was holding my body underwater and I was sinking and no one could hear my screams.

What was happening inside me didn't match what was happening in my house. No shots were even fired. It was an audible flashback triggered by the cop reaching for his clip. Years later, I would have the name for my experience: post-traumatic stress disorder or PTSD. At that moment, however, I did what I had been told to do—just keep quiet, just leave things unsaid. I had been brought up to believe that silence was strength. It would be several years before I was able to be emotionally vulnerable.

"Get out the way!"

He spoke to me as if this shit was normal and I would know what to do. The way he held the holster around the gun reminded me that they were trained killers who had no problem hurting people who look like me or come from my block. I had seen it on TV and in the streets in Toronto. I had seen it in my own hood. Police did not exist to serve and protect. They never had. As far as we knew, the cops came to terrorize and kill people in communities like mine. If you were a Black person (and especially if you were identifiably poor) you were an immediate threat in their eyes. From its beginnings, the police force was built to seek and destroy, not serve and protect. Or if they were serving and protecting, it wasn't neighbourhoods like ours.

I only remember the barrel of a gun. Between the cop entering and leaving my room, it all felt like a blur. I remember the aftermath, though. The house was unrecognizable. Wardrobes on the ground, clothes scattered amongst the broken toys tossed to the floor. There was no clear way to walk without pricking your feet. Some doors were hanging on their hinges, broken from having been forced open too fast. Bins toppled over. Curtains ripped down. It looked as though a storm had hit the house. The tornado of the law had broken it to pieces.

I walked halfway down the stairs and saw only one cop left, signalling the crew outside to leave. They came for something rather than someone, but they left with nothing. My mom talked to that officer for a few minutes. I couldn't quite see her face, but I could hear the crackle in her voice. The rhythmless speech seasoned with pain and humiliation. She did not look shaken up, but I knew she would be. She was my homie. I knew her inside and out. She worked multiple jobs but did everything to spend time with us kids, and she helped us out with reading and homework when she could. She was the queen, and this was her kingdom. I came down, the guardian of the palace, the man of the house as my dad was always at work. I was the youngest, but anyone who would step to my mom would have to step to me.

"I'm deeply sorry, ma'am," the officer uttered quickly, leaving faster than they came.

I peeked down from the staircase and caught a glimpse of her face, wrinkled in confusion. At one point, I wasn't thinking straight and thought they'd come for me. For all the Hubba Bubba chewing gum I stole and flipped for cash at recess, or all the toys I scooped from the department store and traded for bike supplies. Turns out they got the wrong house. Wrong address. Wrong intel. No-knock warrant. And that was it. We were supposed to go back to "normal." The least they could have done was clean up the storm they'd created, though they couldn't have done anything about the bad taste in our mouths.

The poets around me say the eyes are a window to the soul. For most of my life, those windows have been foggy from the stuff brewing inside me. I have had a hard time seeing clearly. I got used to hearing about multiple shootings. I have been near drive-by shootings. This was the norm in my hood and in other blocks like mine around the city. The one and only redeeming thing about Canadian winters is that it keeps people from going outside. There were less shootings than in the summer, but we could easily freeze to death in the snow.

Later that day, sitting on our porch, I caught my brother up on what happened.

"Are we living in a war zone or in a community?" I asked jokingly, thinking I might use humour to lighten the weight of the situation.

Deep down, my brother knew this was not unique to our community. He took a long, somewhat awkward pause, forcing me to think. I would find out somewhere beyond these few city blocks (which was all we knew) that the same shit was happening elsewhere, in other housing projects. But when I was young, it was hard to see beyond the neighbourhood we never left. One of the OGs often talked about *societal norms*. I didn't know what that meant yet, but one day I would learn. I knew the OGs had to do what they had to do to survive. This spirit in me knew the spirit in them. I knew they were geniuses though they could not fully claim it. They were talented and creative, but there weren't many platforms in the neighbourhood for us to showcase it. All we got was the early mornings and late nights. Ten toes down on the street corner.

After a deeply needed time to process, my brother broke the silence.

"Are we living in a war zone or in a community?" he whispered. "Both." And then he walked inside the house, closing the door behind him, leaving me alone on the porch.

It wasn't until years later that I recognized the cop who came into my room. He was the same man who knocked out youth in the alleyways behind the basketball court because we weren't "cooperating" with his harassment. This was the same cop who told us kids that, regardless of how the cops treat us, we had to respect them. This is the opposite of what I learned growing up, the opposite of the rules of the hood: respect is earned, not given. The same cop we knew planted drugs and guns on youth, which was a common practice when cops needed to meet their quota or find someone to blame when they didn't find what they came for. My body recognized him in my room that day before my mind could realize what was going on. I remember hearing his boots when they pressed into the spine of youth who had used the law books to tell the cops what they were doing was wrong. The same hands of "law enforcement" that flew towards my homies as they tried to defend their innocent family members who were unjustly crushed into pieces by police. The same boots on the back of the necks of OGs on the corner who were just enjoying the summer cookout and late-night Dominoes. If they found money in our pockets, they tipped themselves and told us to keep walking.

I did not know everything. I was still learning, still sprouting. But I quickly learned that talk was cheap. How they treated us spoke louder. I could only believe what I saw people do, not what they said. There was a clear separation between the world they came from and the world we lived in. Their words and actions never matched, or if they did, it was never in our favour. One planet. Two worlds.

Next time someone knocks on the door on a Sunday, we ain't opening it. Whether it's the Jehovah's Witnesses or those kids who sell chocolate bars no one ever buys. Either way, we didn't want to talk to any of them. Sundays were reserved for mama dukes, ginger tea, gospel music, and oven bake.

In the time before smartphones, all we had was our word about what happened when we interacted with cops. Later, with the rise of social media, we would have video evidence. But in court, our word and video evidence didn't amount to much. Justice doesn't live in court-rooms. Same shit, different day.

I did not like institutions growing up. Schools. The church. The police. Run by people who had no concept of the neighbourhood, the people, and what went on in our lives. What institutions know about us was limited to the news, which is itself a sea of misinformation, stereotypes, and the criminalization of people based on their postal code and skin colour.

The church up the street was my first beef. The pastor kicked you out if you didn't have your "Sunday best" clothes on. All we had were hoodies and ball shoes. I wondered if the God they were praising approved of what they were doing, using offering money from the poor to buy material things, all the while looking down on Black people and worshipping white folk as if they were God. My brother and I had seen right through their gimmicks.

I didn't know if they were praying harder than us, but in the end, white folk got better cars, owned houses surrounded by medical offices, technology centres, and banks, and lived in neighbourhoods where expensive coffee shops, fitness centres, and healthy grocery stores stocked with non-GMO foods were within walking distance. What I did know is that we lived in the middle of the woods—trying to survive poverty, inadequate housing, underfunded schools with no resources or community programs, not to mention the drug trade. These people who worked in our communities but lived far away from our hood would hold community fundraisers and boast about all the work they'd done to "change lives." But that wasn't the facts. These same people treated us like we were criminals. The idea that being in a community longer gave people a better understanding of a community is flawed. Some teachers, officers, and community leaders have been here forever and still have no clue how the hood is created or the forces that make it what it is. Proximity does not equal understanding. We needed less tears from these people and more floods of justice. Without resources and a proper education, school and the few community programs that did run felt like a prison for many of us.

Money could help with a lot of the things we needed growing up, but it wouldn't be able to heal the trauma. The past was in our shadow. The unhealed wounds would remain. The streams of blood would continue to drip down, leaving a trail on everything in its path. Healing was a distant country I did not know how to get to.

Some of the damage you could see. But because we were young, we couldn't see all of the wounds, the damage, until we were older.

As our blood stained the pavement and our cries for help fell on deaf ears, we understood that the first and primary language of the police was violence. We saw them as a legalized gang. They were paid by the city's budget and taxpayer dollars to bend bodies and get away with it. I've been around the streets long enough to know they weren't only paid by the city . . . many of the corrupt cops we saw lurking were also paid off by the streets.

Any curb server in the hood knows we are a tiny part of the supply chain and the bigger players and suppliers don't live in the hood and never ever come to the hood. Some of those players were never hood people to begin with. Many were corporate business owners, public officials, and people you'd "least" suspect. The biggest police busts never happen in the hood. Most happen in residential communities and on commercial properties where people own their property. The owners of these properties and their affiliates have judges, lawyers, realtors, doctors, accountants, media connections, politicians, cops, and more on payroll. Many cities and small towns across Ontario are run and operated by biker gangs and other organized groups. But the mainstream news doesn't report the truth. The real people moving weight for drugs and money ain't in the hood or from it. They just paint neighbourhoods like mine as the source of everything when in the big picture of things we were a pebble in the ocean of the street game.

According to Toronto Anti-Violence Intervention Strategy (TAVIS), police were being paid millions of dollars to harass, abuse, and arrest us 24 hours a day, especially during the summer when the city enforced a curfew for us. We were prepared for the usual events that followed. My friends were stopped for simply walking and being Black, and when any of us tried to say something the cops would corner us, beat us, hold their hand on their gun, or if there were more witnesses than they liked, target us for future harassment. If boots were being pressed into the necks of youth because the cop felt like it, we had to swallow the echoes of ours screams because the threat of being held at gunpoint was real. Many of the OGs around us fought back in self-defence, but the cops always spun it as assault in their report and sent them to jail. Every time we saw the cops, it was an internal battle for us not to fight back.

Instead of community programs, affordable housing, free mental health services, quality education, or a livable wage, we got TAVIS. Their solution for eradicating poverty was to eradicate us. The message was clear. They didn't see us as human. Our human rights did not matter because such rights did not apply to people that are considered subhuman. *I wondered why those with power and money would spend trillions of dollars to find life on other planets, but at the same time, spend trillions of dollars actively destroying human life in impoverished communities across our own planet. To me, as a child, this was a living contradiction.*

Regardless of the race of the cops, they were always police officers first. It didn't matter if their action was rooted in a misunderstanding, they were never held responsible for stomping on the bodies of youth, shattering lives, or stealing children away from their families. If we did wrong in the hood we got a eulogy, but if a cop did wrong, they got transferred to a new division and received a fat bonus and pension.

Not one of us ever felt served or protected by police, and many of us, in fact, felt the opposite—they did not want us to exist and this was no surprise. I was young and I already sensed the game was rigged. I couldn't articulate it but I knew things did not make sense. How could you oppress others and believe wholeheartedly you are doing the right thing?

Reality is a hard pill to swallow. I've noticed that some people who didn't come from the hood and didn't face these problems personally choose to live in a fictional world where economic and social problems don't exist. This utopic dreamland was not a place I ever wanted to go. I'd rather be here—on my street corner. Ten toes down on the ground.

CITY OF TORONTO BUDGET AND FUNDING

YEAR	SCHOOL OPERATIONS	POLICE
2008	$680 million	$881 million
2009	630 "	917 "
2010	570 "	956 "
2011	660 "	1.00 billion
2012	670 "	1.02 "

Black and Indigenous people murdered by police in Canada

Gedi Ali Gedi
Regis Korchinski-Paquet
D'Andre Campbell
Jamal Francique
Machuar Madut
Clive Mensah
Gregory Ritchie
Olando Brown
Joey Knapaysweet
Illutak Anautak
Adrian Lacquette
Raymond Alliman
Pierre Coriolan
Bony Jean-Pierre
Charles Qirngnirq
Daniel Legarde
Shirley Williams
Jovan Williams
Sandy Michel
Debra Chrisjohn
Abdirahman Abdi
Philippe-Charles Leclerc
Andrew Loku
Rene Gallant
Marc Ekamba-Boekwa
Abdurahman Ibrahim
  Hassan
Abdi Hirsi
Marvel Woodhouse
James McIntyre
James Butters
Kwasi Skene-Peters
Alain Magloire
Naverone Woods
Jermaine Carby

Donald Thompson
Ryan Jacob
Malcolm Jackman
Daniel Charland
Lance Cutarm
Ian Pryce
Frank Anthony Berry
Karen Lander
Michael Eligon
Anthony Murray
Corey Armstrong
Keith Prescod
Angela Lavoie
Bernadette Auger
Romeo Wesley
Eric Osawe
Reyal Jensen Jardine-
  Douglas
Alexander Manon
Eugene Knight
Douglas Heagle
David Fetterly
John Simon
Harry Haineault
Jacqueline Montgrand
Kenneth Standingready-
  McKay
Walid Maragan
Byron Debassaagie
Quilem Registre
Dwayne Dustyhorn
Oumar Thiam
Alwy Nadhir
Delbert Pelletier
Shelton McKenzie

Duane Christian
Dennis St. Paul
Howard Fleury
Matthew Dumas
Zunga Bashir
Adeyeri Robinson
Rohan Wilson
Courtney Peters
Jerry Knight
O'Brien Christopher-Reid
Sugston Brookes
Peter Lamonday
Deng Fermino Kuol
Clark Whitehouse
Chevranna Abdi
Ramsey Whitefish
Donald Miless
Danny Sand
Melvin Bigsky
Keldon McMillan
Maurice Linklater
Henry Musaka
Hugh Dawson
Wayne Rick Williams
Andrew Bramwell
Tommy Anthony Barnett
Dudley George
Albert Moses
Ian Clifford Coley
Raymond Lawrence
Michael Wade Lawson
Lester Donaldson
Albert Johnson
Buddy Evans
Garfield Belfon

To our brothers and sisters that we lost in Canada, the United States, and globally, we do this work in memory of you. We hold all your families, friends, and loved ones in our prayers. We remember your names to honour you and to keep your memory alive as we continue to fight for justice and accountability. May you forever rest in power.

The Flip

A startup is a human institution designed to create a new product or service under conditions of extreme uncertainty.

—Eric Ries

You can't use up creativity. The more you use, the more you have.

—Maya Angelou

Age 11: I sat on the front porch, in the middle of the red brick housing complex, with my fists clenched, the sunlight beaming through the broken streetlights above my head reflecting off the tears rippling down my cheeks. I took a few deep breaths and the stale air invaded my lungs. Five minutes earlier, I had left my bike on the porch and run upstairs to change into shorts and a tank top. As I rode back from my morning trip to Price Chopper, with four grocery bags on each handlebar and an old JanSport backpack hanging on by a thread, I thought: "Grocery runs for five people will be the death of me." My new clothes were already drenched in sweat.

Quickly packing everything away for my family, I crunched up the remaining shopping bags into a ball and stored them in the large bag under the sink, as usual. The second I went back outside I noticed my bike was gone. My single-speed BMX with its ruby red front and back pegs. Kidnapped. It was the only thing I'd ever owned. The only thing in the world that was mine. My dad had given it to me as a gift, and I had cherished it for two short years. Now it was gone, and I'd never be able to get another bike after that. At that moment, I knew I couldn't tell my parents that someone had stolen my bike. I needed to find another way to get around instead of being forced to walk a marathon all day every day. I did errands every week and walking for hours was not an option. So, I did the wise thing any kid on the block would do—I created a solution to the problem.

"ICE CREAM!"

I could hear the bells from an incoming ice cream truck just behind my house. They always sounded creepy to me, but all the kids ran like someone stole their lunch money. Stopping outside 52, the neighbourhood basketball court, the truck driver switched to real music. Hip hop music. Tupac's "Changes," my favourite song, my personal anthem, came blaring out the ice cream truck window. Pac gave us social and political power, and helped me understand that we are not the cause of what happens when forced into dire circumstances—we are the effect.

Hip hop speaks the truth. It was my outlet. A therapeutic escape from the daily experiences of poverty, racism, violence, and exclusion that I felt in society. Hip hop is a language to express what trauma and systemic oppression look like and how it can be overcome. It taught me how to value and understand my streets and it painted the world's most beautiful pictures with its storytelling. As a celebration of resilience, music taught me more truth about the world than school ever did.

As I stood up from my porch and looked around the corner of my house to see all the hype, I noticed a little kid. Just as I saw her, the wind picked up and stole the scoop of chocolate ice cream right off her cone. As it fell swiftly to the ground, her eyes began to water. By the time it splat on the uneven concrete she was bawling.

My heart grew heavy for the young queen. But what the ice cream truck driver did next was genius. He called her over with her dad—and replaced the cone! I said to myself, free cone . . . free bike. I had an idea. Where could I get bikes for cheap?

"Yoooooooooooo Imeeeeeee!" I yelled. "Reach my crib in two hours!"

Imee was my homie. I rolled with him anytime I had a plan. I sprinted two kilometres down the Warden Avenue strip to Danforth Avenue. There, I saw a cheap bike locked up; the same model I had ridden every day for the last few years, rusted chain . . . and barely used by its owner. . . .

I cut the lock with a bolt cutter I'd taken from my dad's tool kit earlier and rode the bike home on its flat tires. I arrived in my backyard and started fixing it up with tools that I found at home or borrowed from neighbours. I patched the holes in both tires, cleaned and oiled the chain, centred the handlebars, and took off the stickers. Just in time for Imee's arrival.

My dad had taught me how to ride, fix, and maintain bikes. Though my brothers and I rarely spent time with him, given that he worked factory shifts day and night, when we did see him, he was always de-termined to make bikes a part of our lives. We never quite understood why, but it felt like his life's purpose to teach us. His engaging lessons made physical activity and affordable travel fun. Giving me my red ruby was our only connection.

"Remember that bike by DQ?" I asked him.

"Five-finger discount and a lil reno. Let's flip it!" he replied.

This wasn't just revenge for my bike getting stolen. Losing my bike had given me an idea for a business opportunity. And if I got Imee on board as a business partner, all the other kids would join because we were the ringleaders—we could get others to join our missions quite easily. Dr. Alex, our childhood homie, had left the hood unexpectedly, moving to some other housing project in the west end of the city. One August, just a week before school started, we rolled up on our bikes and found his house empty, not even any curtains on the windows. The front door was unlocked and wide open and his entire family was gone. Our block would never be the same, but we had to carry on his legacy. Youngins on the block looked up to us because when we hustled together or did anything to make money, we did as the OGs taught us: we fed our crew and left no one hungry.

We were already flipping things for cash—as inspired by the local drug dealers—but I wanted to provide a different kind of business.

In our neighbourhood, we had limited bikes, and usually only one or two "hood" bikes, owned and operated by the entire community 24/7/365. In other words, it was our neighbourhood bike sharing service, allowing anyone to use community bikes for running errands. When we were finished with the errands, we brought the bike back to the basketball court. If we returned the bike late, we would hear it from the next person waiting in line. This is what bike share looked like before city bike sharing programs became a popular global phenomenon. The lineups for the bike were always long, sometimes you'd have to wait two hours, so I decided to create a better option. I started collecting old bikes with the intention of fixing them up and flipping them for more than I paid. I would sell people bikes at a low cost. If people didn't have the money, they paid in food or rented the bike by the hour. I would be the supplier, but this time I wasn't dropping off drugs—I was dropping off bikes.

To me, the bike was my life. It took me everywhere my pockets couldn't. I had no money for bus fare. It was also my fitness workout and a way to escape the drugs, school, over-policing, and limited community programs that left me bored and stranded on the street corner in the neighbourhood. But now my bike was gone. I knew I had to convince Imee. I knew getting a bike wouldn't be enough. I needed to have a plan for him to see. Visual, audio, and hands-on. So I began to sketch it in the dirt between our feet. I drew a rectangle to represent his backyard and split it into four even areas.

Taking the bike back out of Imee's hand, I said, "This will be the first bike shop on the block." I broke it down for him. Area one: a mechanic shop with tools to get bikes road ready. Areas two and three: for damaged and broken bikes and parts, as well as bikes that needed simple maintenance. Area four: a lounge area to handle money transactions.

We had all the tools we needed from the neighbourhood. We already knew we could get free busted bikes at different Scarborough garbage bins. But we would also need some newer bikes—not brand new, but new enough to provide a solid foundation we could build upon.

"We'll scoop 'free' bikes," I whispered. "Borrow the ones people won't miss. Fix 'em up then flip 'em."

"Make money? Engineer flex and help out the block? Say no more!" Imee said, smiling cheek to cheek. Imee would do waves with his eyebrows when he knew I was going somewhere that he wanted to go.

With his head nodding up and down on repeat, my homie had now accepted his role as business partner. Within 24 hours of having my bike stolen, I'd stolen an abandoned bike, sketched a business plan in the dirt, and convinced a close friend to join me in my enterprise. To Imee, it wasn't the words but the drawing that made hope visible for him. We realized that the real problem wasn't the lack of sharable hood bikes. The real problem was the food deserts, aka food apartheid, and grocery stores that were a 60–90 minute walk away. Youth like me were sent on grocery runs and had to spend huge amounts of time on this family responsibility.

The bike shop was our way to improve access for families in need. We couldn't physically move the grocery store to the community, but we could bring the people closer to it. In one day, we "borrowed" two bikes. By the end of the week we had 20—all old and broken but fixable. In two weeks, we were fully operational in my friend's backyard. A bike shop with quick turnaround times, from request to delivery, that provided low-cost bikes. Bike frames and tires on the grass. Mechanics on my left and right, fixing bikes to get them road ready. I was the CEO and, with Imee, co-founder. We had six third graders as mechanics-in-training, learning how to build a bike from scratch, as well as how to fix flats and change tubes. These interns were unpaid until they proved they mastered the skills and could build a bike from scratch. We had four staff members between Grades 4 and 6 who always got their cut as they needed to help out at home financially— food, medication, clothing, whatever their families needed.

Now it was my turn to pass on my knowledge and skills to the younger ones. I had natural entrepreneurial skills and a passion for running my own business, like the street dealers who taught us how to flip things for cash. This offered us tangible things to change our reality, something school didn't give us at the time. Our street culture was to eat with those you starved with, so we took care of each other. If your people were hungry, you fed them or found a way to help. If you had extra, you would always share. And if you could, you'd teach them how to fish—that is, a way to make money and never go hungry. Coming up on the block, the *WE* was the motive and the *I* was secondary.

We had some hiccups early on in our start-up organization. Some bikes were too small for our buyers and people wanted customizations (size, colour, and sticker decals). So we increased the number of new bikes coming in and adjusted the business accordingly, pivoting quickly. We also offered to fix flats free of charge with a customer's first purchase. We provided more bikes at a low cost, helping community members improve their level of fitness, access distant grocery stores, and lessen transportation times. Not having to pay expensive transit fares also meant less expenses overall. With all of this, we had officially launched our local business. We were children taking matters into our own hands.

For decades, the government's failed promises to improve the hood left us without afterschool and community programs—failed promises and apologies were just normal practice in the hood. Instead they gave us a few stereotypical basketball court installations and strategic photo ops for politicians that didn't change anything for us. We still had nowhere to go after the school bell rang. These weren't solutions to help us eat.

These experiences taught me that we need to know and care about the people we are designing things for if we want to create meaningful products and innovation. This led me to test-run a bike shop and then turn it into a local backyard business. By the community for the community.

My bike shop was the first of many experiences that taught me *how to lose, "take the L," and bounce back*. What started off as stealing for revenge turned into a small business born out of empathy for our neighbours. As kids, we didn't really know how to define the thinking process we had used to launch our business. For us, it was our natural way of thinking, to use our creativity and resourcefulness to survive. Years later, we would discover a term for the type of creativity we'd used to set up our successful bike shop. We called it hustling, but outside the hood, they called it **Design Thinking**.

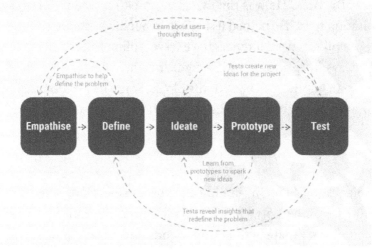

DESIGN THINKING: A NON-LINEAR PROCESS

Teo Yu Siang and Interaction Design Foundation

If I was to break down how we did what we did, it would go like this:

1. **Empathize** – Know, understand, and care about users. Gain insights into community (people and needs).
2. **Define** – Define a core problem to be solved.
3. **Ideate** – Generate ideas that explore numerous possibilities for solving the problem. There is no right answer; think outside of the box.
4. **Prototype** – Build and learn by doing. Try out ideas and determine which ones to accept, re-examine, improve, or reject.

5. **Test** – Go into the real world and test prototypes. Use feedback from users to make adjustments. Refine and improve the building of the prototype.
6. **Repeat** – Repeat the entire process until the prototype meets the needs of the community.

In my eyes, we were developing highly transferable skills in entrepreneurship and design—skills that could be applied to bigger and more legit endeavours. I had done it in remembrance of my childhood homie, Dr. Alex. He was the living and breathing figure of hope and inspiration to us. He helped us believe in ourselves and in the idea that the possibilities were limitless if we were willing to fail again and again and always keep trying until we got it right. This was my chance to bring some motivation back to the block. Some inspiration that might let another rose grow from the broken, blood-stained pavement.

Our biggest problem in running our businesses as kids was managing money: we didn't know how to invest our profits and grow them for the long-term. That summer, my friends and I made money hustling and flipping things for cash, but at the end of the summer we had nothing to show for it. The more cash that came in, the faster it disappeared. We had no records of where it went and didn't have the discipline yet to work smart, not just hard. Schools hadn't taught us about financial literacy or provided access to entrepreneurial resources. Instead they gave us worksheets that taught us nothing other than how to vomit out the information they'd just given us.

"Billy lives on a farm. He has three apples and gets two more from his apple tree. How many apples does Billy have?" In Grade 1, laughing at this question got me sent to the office, but as a city kid, worksheets and farms weren't challenging me to learn and they weren't relevant to the world I lived in. Somedays felt like a waste of time, but if they had given us what we needed, they might have given us another option, a way out of financial illiteracy. What might I have dreamed of if I'd learned how to manage money as a kid . . . if I knew how to register a legal business, understood accounting, or how to run a business operation from home? I was young, but I knew there was information we needed that we did not have access to—and that we would have to find it on our own. I wanted to work smart, not just hard. D. Watkins in *We Speak for Ourselves* was right to say that "Access to information is class based." Without this information, we were fighting a war we couldn't see. We were in an economic and social prison. School taught us how to be good employees: Follow the rules. Stay within the mould. Walk in line. Hands up. Hands down. Obey the bell. And if you didn't follow the rules, you got punished. In the words of Angela Davis: "When children attend schools that place a greater value on discipline and security than on knowledge and intellectual development, they are attending prep schools for prison."

As kids, our minds naturally think across multiple subject areas, but the traditional focus at school is one subject at a time. Straight lines without deviation. What we needed were teachers and mentors to help us rediscover our own stories and reclaim our genius.

Teachers with zero cultural understanding of who we were and no experience teaching in the hood were destroying more lives than they were helping. Millions of kids were sent to their death daily—mentally, emotionally, spiritually, and educationally. Pushing us into courses below our ability, targeting us with low expectations, disproportionately suspending and expelling us—all things to make us feel both hyper visible and invisible at the same time. Years later, I would graduate from teachers college at Ontario Tech University and go on to examine programs across the country. I discovered that many of these programs were ill-equipped and designed to fail us before we'd even learned to tie our shoes. Like being freshly released from prison, in school and the streets, I felt free but not free at the same time. In school, they treated us like inmates in classroom seats. It was a prep school for the big house.

Schools expelling and suspending rather than listening. Cops arresting and brutally assaulting the homies they've planted drugs on.

Governments approving cuts to community initiatives. It all sent the message that *we were trespassing on earth* and did not have a right to life. Living in my neighbourhood, it was common for a million things to negatively impact our mental health at the same time. There was never enough time to process any of it. Every day, things happened to us and all around us. We didn't have time to think, let alone breathe. Somedays felt impossible.

It took me ten years to locate the memories of why we closed our bike shop forever that fall of 2004. I remember we were in the bike shop when we heard a crash. It sounded like the smashing of a car windshield. We ran over to the circle building and saw a middle-aged woman. Whether she fell or jumped we did not know. I was sorry for the children running away after having seen the body spread out on the pavement. I wasn't there to see the impact, but the aftermath was more than enough to take in—the body, spread across the parking lot, deformed and unrecognizable. She must have fallen from the top floor of the circle building, bouncing off the car and onto the pavement. Some things you cannot unsee. Especially when you are a child. And the pain just kept coming that year.

One day in March, on the day of my 11th birthday, there was an apparent home invasion in an apartment building and shots were fired. Our community leader, Blue Boy, was stolen from us. Metal shells penetrated his body and chewed his flesh as the shells skipped across the apartment floor. Wrong place, wrong time.

Blue had been the most respected community leader in the neighbourhood. He worked as a neighbourhood camp counsellor and tutor and always took care of his family, which included not just his siblings but all the kids in our hood. He was the definition of what it meant to be selfless. He was the sun that gave us light when it was dark. With him, we believed we could be something more than what was set out in front of us. We lost a pillar of hope in our community. And I would never celebrate my birthday again. Blue Boy's presence gave me hope. His smile was one of peace, his laughter one of joy. He was a true gift for us in the present, but now his presence was gone. It was a day that changed my life and our community forever. From making memories to becoming a memory. Without him, hope was gone.

It was normal for us kids to think of getting the person who took him from us because we knew the cops wouldn't do anything. But we also knew that revenge wouldn't bring Blue Boy back.

Our lives were now empty, without meaning. Cold, numb. People were starting to disappear. And before we'd even had a chance to process his life and his death and what he meant to the block, another life was up in the balance the same year.

One summer day, several of us kids were at Woodbine Beach on a camp trip with the thousands of other kids that flooded the shores of Lake Ontario every day all summer long. We were playing in the sand and swimming in the water when counsellors, lifeguards, and block kids noticed Isaiah was missing. Twelve minutes later, after a coast to coast search, they found him in the water. He had no vital signs. They pulled him out of the lake and brought him back using CPR, and then rushed him to the Hospital for Sick Children in critical condition. He was in a coma for two months and likely suffered brain damage as he was denied oxygen, which would impair his vision and motor skills. But he was strong and we were sure he was going to make it. When we found out he didn't, we were all shattered; his family, his friends, and the whole neighbourhood. We remembered his bright smile, his joy, his infectious laugh. He was one of those people whose presence alone brought light and hope to every space he was in. He was only eight years old and gone before he had a chance to live a full life.

The church on the block told me and my homies to just pray about it, but that didn't help. It was not possible to pray away trauma. The pain was as real as the street corners we lived on. My heart was heavy and my eyes were worn out. It was hard to stomach a life where my people were starting to disappear. It was hard to swallow the reality that my fam, friends, and the people I was coming up with were dying young, before they had the chance to find their purpose. Despite starting my own bike shop at 11 years old, losing my people made 2004 the worst year of my life. We lost Blue Boy, Isaiah, and a mother. I didn't realize it at the time, but the losses, pain, and trauma were just getting started. In my hood, death was no stranger. By the time 15 lives were stolen from us by the streets of Toronto, all before my 12th birthday, I stopped counting. I wanted to hide myself from the reality of what was going on.

The resulting trauma and pain we carried with us ironically created a bond between many of us friends, family, and community members—a bond forged through our collective pain and collective silence. I just wish we had moved differently. Instead of suffering in silence and bonding through secrecy, I imagined a world where we came together through the pursuit of healing, of being vulnerable. There was always a danger in being emotionally open about stuff that happened to us or around us. Sometimes just opening up about something in our family or community would break bonds. Bonds that were only created through pain and a refusal to look at what hurt us. Many families around me lived by the motto: *Don't talk about family business.* Some people were silent about pain just to "keep the peace."

Our past held us hostage.

Some days we broke down walls and other days it felt like the walls were caving in. This was my life and the life of those around me. The life of many of us in housing. Like many, I lost interest in the things that once made me happy.

That year, things changed. The bike shop was no more and looking back it all made sense. There was no time to process and recover from the impact.

Growing up, we didn't have or know about national support services like Kids Help Phone—a 24/7 free and confidential professional counselling and information service that uses phone, text, mobile app, and a website to help young people through challenging times—or organizations like Black Youth Helpline.

As a kid, I never knew the meaning or importance of mental health. These words were alien to our community. Even if we did understand it, we still didn't have the people to talk to, judgment-free, about mental health, trauma, depression, anxiety, or even suicidal thoughts. In my adulthood, I was happy to see organizations like Kids Help Phone and Black Youth Helpline become accessible to young people across the country in their time of need. Sometimes, like many around me, I felt that the stuff I saw and the issues I carried could not be fixed. We had stone cold exteriors, but what we really needed was just someone to talk to.

I wonder what could happen if our mental health was better supported by communities? To give us time to think, to process, and to heal. How much more would we be able to learn?

Hip hop often gets blamed for all the social issues that poverty creates. But when I look beyond the stereotypical images and language, the experiences expressed through hip hop culture are ones I share. I see hip hop as a tool for looking deeper—a therapeutic storytelling of the artist's life, reporting where they are from and what they see. Hip hop is a tool to fight back and have our voices heard.

Amidst all the traumas and triumphs, laughter and pain, the only thing that kept me going at this point in my life was my mother . . . and hip hop music. My two roses in the uneven concrete.

British
Columbia

Location: *Hope, British Columbia (5669 km from Halifax)*
2:00 p.m.: *Eastbound to Africville, Halifax, Nova Scotia*

After leaving Vancouver and cycling for a few days, I was ready to quit and go back home. I wanted to take an airplane back to Scarborough and enjoy my summer. Maybe even hit up Caribana with the mandem—a term we use to describe the homies. I wanted to be stress-free. My eyes were bloodshot red and my eyelids were struggling to stay open. But if I went to sleep, I would sleep for months. I could never let the team know what was going through my mind as I didn't want them to have doubts about the entire movement.

Addisiane and I stopped our bikes on the shoulder of Highway 5 in British Columbia and tried to catch our breath. We were officially halfway towards our city destination of Merritt, cycling up the Coquihalla Highway.

The Coquihalla is a 200 kilometre-long highway and is one of the worst roads in all of North America in the wintertime. Cycling up the highway, I quickly realized why. I was used to the flat, urban highways of Toronto, but this was a mountainous highway. We were literally on roads that went over a mountain. Hundreds upon hundreds of fatal accidents happened on the Coquihalla and it all made sense. You had to know how to drive out here or things could get ugly really fast.

"You good?" I asked Addisiane, while grabbing my bottle to see how much water was left.

"Naw, you good?" he said, staring at the ground like a deflated balloon.

We were riding up this highway on a steady incline. We didn't see a flat road for the first 30 km and the map told us that we had roughly 18 km more to go, uphill, before we got to a more manageable elevation. At the turtle pace we were going, we'd been riding for hours. My hamstrings were spaghetti. I felt like they would rip at any moment. Each pedal felt like it would trigger a muscle cramp that would last for the whole day. Though I had trained for nine months prior, nothing could have prepared me to do this trip with little or no sleep over the past year.

"Yo CC I'm out. You got water?" he asked, stretching out his hand in my direction.

"Say no more," I replied, giving him the last bit of water I had left.

The first day of the ride we talked a lot, but today we didn't. We were too tired and we had to use all our energy to focus on not getting hit by cars or dying of thirst. Addi's water was supposed to last him two hours, but he was literally a dehydrated dog. And it was 30+ degrees Celsius and the sun was still heating up. The water in my bottle was gone in the snap of a finger and all I had left to consume was candy and fruit. My trusty bike jersey had three built-in pockets on the back so I could easily reach for my skittles, fuzzy peaches, bananas, granola bars—and my iPhone and portable charger—while cycling, so I could eat on the go. We had 120 km to cycle today, but we were only doing an average of 25 km/h. Usually we'd be able to do this in about five hours without stops, but because of the hills, we had to stop it seemed like every ten minutes and we were running low on food and water. Though the sun was winning, we hopped back on our bikes and continued cycling up the Coquihalla.

Addisiane was 22 years old, born and raised in Havelock, just east of Peterborough, Ontario. I'd never heard of it, but I knew it was a small, predominantly white town with a population of 4500. Even though he didn't grow up with the lessons from the hood, he always took it upon himself to learn about things he didn't learn in school. We met the previous year at a sports camp and resort called Muskoka Woods. I was a staff coach and Addisiane worked alongside children with disabilities. On the basketball court, we shared the desire to win. Winning was the only option, and we wouldn't go home until we won a game. Outside of sports, his plan was to join the army and move to Halifax, so I didn't know if I would see him again after the ride was over. But I knew he was a special part of the team. Without Addisiane, the ride might not have happened. In the early stages, when it was just a sketched idea on a piece of paper, he kept me motivated. He believed in me during the first months when nothing was working out. We grew up in different neighbourhoods with complete opposite realities but he was still a real one.

Above our heads, the mountains pierced through the cotton candy clouds sprinkled through the baby blue skies. We were surrounded in every direction by evergreen forest that hugged the mountains, roads, hiking trails, and wildlife in her arms. Eagles were gliding in the sky with no care in the world. Deer, bears, and moose were chilling along the edges of the forest and beside the clear blue lakes, and I swear all the trees looked a hundred feet tall minimum. I used to dream of seeing mountains and now here they were in real life. The scenery made my heart skip a beat. I felt hypnotized and at the same time so peaceful. Compared to the gangs of wild raccoons, squirrels, and pigeons that stalked and attacked people in Toronto, this was like a little bit of heaven . . . until l snapped back to reality. Driving through the mountains and looking out the passenger window at the views was dope, like in the movies. But cycling all day up the sides of a mountain in a heat wave was not like driving. I needed to be more focused on survival than sightseeing. Wearing a skintight bike suit like all long-distance cyclists made us aerodynamic, but it didn't seem to help much as we were going uphill. Mountains. Mountains. Mountains.

"Truckkkkkk!" Addisiane screamed, cycling 40 metres behind me.

The highway shoulder started to get pretty small. On this stretch, it was two or three feet wide. One foot to our right was a tiny guardrail that couldn't have saved us if we fell off our bikes. On the other side of the guardrail was a cliff; the trees and rocks at the bottom of that cliff were the only thing to catch us if we fell over. Two feet to our left were cars and 40 foot long trucks zooming by at 120 km/h. At any given moment we could get hit by a truck or fall off a cliff. Without our sunglasses, we would have already gone blind from the rocks that the speeding trucks had pitched at our heads as they flew by. So the goal each day was to stay alive. Every moment we had to stay alert.

Rocks weren't the only problem. After the trucks flew by, the wind gusts from their aftermath would shake our thin road bike tires. They quivered in the wind, threatening to blow us into traffic or over the cliff. Our cycling shoes were clipped into our bike pedals, which sometimes made it difficult for us to clip out of them in time if we needed to stop on a dime or fight the wind to keep our balance. Things were getting challenging, so we decided to stop and call the support van. We had no more water and were fresh out of snacks. The remaining skittles in my back pocket were now straight liquid. We looked at our phones and then at each other as we realized we had no cell phone bars. No phone signal. No service.

We crawled our way up the highway, taking breaks every couple of kilometres until we got a couple bars of service. This was our only way to call the support van to refill the cold water, Gatorade, and bananas and reload the solid skittles. As we rode, I started to talk to myself in my head. *What is a kid from Scarborough doing out here? Am I in over my head?* I didn't tell Addisiane, but my mind was playing games with me.

I pulled over onto the side of the highway and sat on the guardrail away from traffic. Addisiane looked hurt. Both of his knees were swollen and we couldn't recognize where his knee cap was. In just a few days, he went from having marathon runner's legs to Marshawn Lynch's NFL running back legs. He was no longer white because he didn't use sunscreen. He looked like a red rocket cruising on his bike.

As my mind started to quit on me, I quickly reminded myself of my hood. I couldn't go home at this point. I was already here. I trained. I made a commitment. I couldn't let down the hundreds of people on my team and the millions of kids and families that looked like me from Toronto, Canada, and around the world. Quitting wasn't an option.

Looking down at my cell phone, I saw one bar of cell service, then two. I walked a couple steps up and down the shoulder of the highway to sustain the signal when suddenly a notification popped up on my screen from a newly made Instagram account called *Cheersforcurtis*. Clicking onto the page, I saw that it was filled with short video posts from children and youth from my block. They were sending messages to cheer me on, telling me to keep riding for them as they felt like they were riding with me. The voices of the youth reminded me that this ride was never about me. I was doing it for the kids and for the people. Going forward, every day before starting to cycle, I would take a few minutes to dedicate the ride to a neighbourhood, kid, youth, family, or parent, and I would highlight a community story. This dedication kept our team grounded and reminded them that the ride was not about me and the movement was not about the ride. The ride was just a vehicle. The focus was the stories. Stories of real people who would still be here in the hood after the Ride for Promise was over.

Looking up from my iPhone, I noticed the support van a hundred metres ahead of us, parked at a truck stop on the side of the highway. Addisiane and I hopped on our bikes and cycled as fast as we could towards Cameron and Jarrett, who were waving their hands into the sky so we could recognize them. We made it to the van and refreshed our food and water.

On social media, we looked organized and well planned. But behind the scenes, we were just figuring out things as we went along. There were no solid plans. We just woke up, cycled all day, and hoped we got to the next city in time for dinner so we could eat, speak about our ride to a local audience, and sleep. Then we would wake up and do it all over again until we made it to the hospital or to the finish line in Halifax. I had no idea what came next, so I just focused on one pedal at a time, one bottle of water at a time, and one day at a time. I knew if I focused on one pedal at a time, I would get there eventually.

We got back onto the road to Merritt, British Columbia, but this time we were even more careful. There still weren't designated bike lanes. It was the same three-foot shoulder of the highway we were accustomed to. For some reason, the shoulder only seemed to get smaller as we rode along. Whether it was falling off a cliff or getting hit by a truck, death was a matter of inches. This was new to Addisiane, but for me, being close to death was something I was used to. Riding a bike uphill was light work compared to what we went through coming up. In neighbourhoods like mine, we were literally one or two decisions away from going down a path that led to being arrested, jailed, stolen from our families, or even shot, whether we were involved with street stuff or not. Wrong place wrong time was a real curse.

The Drop

Age 11: I have never met a person in the projects who was born with the thought to sell drugs or hold a gun. When life happens, circumstances drive decisions. In many cases, a lack of opportunity makes risky options seem viable. Sometimes a lack of money drives us to do things we ain't proud of. From the outside, it's easy to judge people for selling poison or living recklessly, but there is a context for everything.

Survival by any means was a general rule for many of those around me. Especially when our stomachs were empty for a few days or we could not get a job.

"Dissolve the powder in hot water. Add baking soda. Boil to separate out the solids. Cool the separated mixture. Cut up the solids into rocks. Wrap for shipment. Package the amounts for sale. Got it?"

Hood chemistry.

I was 11 when I saw my first crack rock and sold my first drug.

After picking the lock to the backdoor of Chris' house, I tiptoed into his living room. The old door screeched. My plan was to sneak up on Chris—my childhood friend—while he was playing video games, but when I looked at his shoe rack, his scuffed up black-on-black Air Force 1s and his parents' steel toe boots were missing. I knew his parents were at work so I assumed he was already outside somewhere riding his bike. But before running back outside, I overheard some voices in the kitchen. I floated over towards the conversation to investigate. With one eye, I peeked around the corner of the kitchen entrance and saw Dre, Chris' older brother. On his right, the dinner table was covered. Pre-packaged weed (it was 2004, way before marijuana was beginning to be legalized around the world) and crack rocks for sale by the hundreds. It looked like the hood version of Costco. They were pushing mad weight. The floor was covered with stacks of cash wrapped in rubber bands by the dozens. The six thickest stacks were all hundreds. The rest were 50s and 20s. I wanted to grab a stack and run it through my fingers from the top bill to the bottom and estimate the amount, but I didn't want to blow my cool. Without them knowing, I watched the science and math lesson Dre led for the rookie curb servers. He showed them the ins and outs of the industry. This was the street curriculum we inherited from the previous generation: how to create and package the product, and how to manage inventory, shipments, financials, risk management, and burner phones. When I walked into Chris' house unannounced, there was always some shit going down. This day was no different.

When employers didn't get back to you, and schools were all too happy to push you out, and your pockets were full of lint, it was the streets that hugged you. Nobody else gave the mandem jobs, so the street employed us. The streets showed us love when our empty fridge was hurting our self-esteem, or when our parents lost their jobs due to, ironically, work-related injuries, leaving us with no other choice but to help out at home. The streets were compassionate when we were unable to pay rent, college or university tuition, dentist bills, or keep the lights and heat on, or buy school clothes, medication, groceries, or sports equipment. They took us in like family and protected us from outsiders. They made sure our stomachs were never empty. At the time, they gave us friendship and a sense of individual responsibility and purpose. And, of course, they gave us money to help with our situation in the immediate sense. The streets gave us something that school did not. Some of those around me really risked it all to feed their children or pay the bills.

Between the high school dropouts, people going to jail, and our homies dying, it was hard to think about the future. We were just living day to day. And today was no different. My motive: food. My stomach was empty, fighting itself, making sounds I'd never heard before. Screaming in confusion, it was unsure of its last fill. My mouth dry, yearning for an ocean.

"*I wanna make money! I gotta eat!*" I yelled, walking into the kitchen in full swagger mode.

Standing in the middle of the doorway I planted my feet firmly and pushed out my chest. With my head held high, I took my hands out of my pockets, closing one fist and covering it with my off hand. They knew who I was; they knew I was a dealer. My inventory was Hubba Bubba gum from Dollarama, bikes and bike parts from people's backyards, and sometimes cars. I stole products and flipped them for cash. I was the human version of the video game Grand Theft Auto: San Andreas. I was the main character CJ from San Andreas and the active look-out for the block. I relayed information to community members daily, reporting on what I saw: licence plate numbers that came through the block, what people looked like, who they visited and how long they stayed, divisional numbers on police cruisers and badge numbers, when they came, why, and for how long. I was the real neighbourhood watch, protecting the block from strangers and police who came during the day to harass people and smash our heads in at night. The police even called us names that were historically used during slavery. It didn't matter if you were selling or not, or if you were a kid or an adult; you existed, and to them, that was a crime. They were there to protect and serve the rich and terrorize poor Black and brown people. *This was the norm.*

I had been in this role since I was six, and in return for my service—keeping a bird's-eye view of the block—I'd developed a photographic memory. But now I wanted to make money. I was hungry for real food, not food bank food, today. That stuff was free, and useful, but sometimes the stuff tasted funny or was expired.

Dre's eyes lit up, and he cracked a smile. He instructed the curb servers to show me the ropes. They were all high school freshman, babies compared to Dre, who had been in the game for over a decade. I learned the ins and outs of the business.

I was now ready for Day One as a runner.

When it came to street operations and the organizational structure of the people involved, it all felt very much like a major institution, like a school or a corporation, with its chain of command. The government ran the schools, they were the suppliers or the plug. Next there were principals and vice-principals, then teachers, educational assistants, secretaries, students, and janitors. The corporate world was the same but different. They had their owners, CEOs, Board of Directors, general managers, coordinators, staff, and the person who delivered the mail. And the streets—different, yet the same. Like wealthy elites, drug dealers too avoided taxes on their earnings, the difference being, on the streets, business risks include your life—imprisonment or death.

My dad often worked out of the city, so I didn't really see him much other than when he brought us money, food, or clothes. He was always working but I never knew where. I assumed it was at a factory somewhere as that's what many of my friends' parents were doing. My mom had worked multiple jobs, night and day, until finally being forced to take time off. I thought she'd gotten laid off or maybe injured. The real cues were the decreasing amounts of store-bought groceries and increasing amounts of food bank food. The bags under her eyes were looking heavier, heavy like *ten days without sleep* heavy. At the time, this was normal. My brothers and I never spent much time with each other and in many ways we were strangers in the same household. Flipping through family photos, it looked like we hung out a lot before I started grade school but I couldn't remember any of that without the photo album. Now we were older, and they were always out with their friends or trying to get a job or find new ways to make money to help out at home. I knew it was time for me to be the man of the house and contribute . . . at least until they decided to come home.

Within a few hours, I had dropped off a few dime bags of weed at two buildings on Danforth Ave. I was not prepared for the crack game, but in my mind, I was ready for a promotion. I hadn't gotten much money yet, but I was feeling some type of way. My heart was racing. I was walking with my chest up. I had a fresh swagger in my step. I was ready to be more vocal when people talked shit to me. I felt like a new person, a child but also a man . . . or at least what I thought a man was. I had some responsibility but now it was time to eat good. To get paid.

Just after sunset, in the parking lot at the back of my crib, Dre gave me a backpack and two simple rules: "Do not be late" and "Do not open the bag." I threw on the Jansport backpack and cycled out of the neighbourhood, down the main strip of Warden Avenue. I rode in style, en route to the convenience store on my single-speed BMX bike with pegs on the front and back wheels, my red rocket. I raced the 69 Warden South bus down the hill and took a right on Danforth. I arrived two minutes early.

Hiding in the alleyway behind the convenience store, and with time to spare, it was all too easy to break rule number two. Taking the backpack off, I quickly looked around to ensure I was alone. With my ashy knuckles, I opened up the zipper to reveal a black plastic bag. Moving it side to side, I saw those same money stacks I saw that morning. I closed the bag then quickly opened it again. Taking the money bag out, I thought I noticed what was at the bottom—a handgun. I had seen one before.

I closed the bag in a hurry. But I closed it too fast to 100 percent confirm what I saw. There was no turning back. I had to make the drop. *Was this for protection? Did this catch a body? Was it about to? Would I be connected? What if I didn't do the drop?* The last minute felt like an hour. My heart rate increased with each car that drove by. My chest was ready to explode. Just before I could put the bag back on my back a car pulled up. Someone inside picked up the bag, and then they were gone.

It all happened so fast I could barely remember the car pulling up and driving off. I took off, racing. I couldn't hear anything, as if I'd gone deaf. A block away from the hood, a police cruiser stopped at the red traffic light just behind me. Suddenly my hearing came back, my heart blowing up my eardrums. I raced up the hill and made a break for it down the sidewalk. A hundred metres until freedom. As I gave a final glance over my shoulder, the police sirens began to scream. The smell of burnt rubber invaded my nose. I watched them closely out of the corner of my eye. As they approached me, I held my breath. Suddenly, they flew right by me. It was my lucky day. Gasping for air, I slowed down to a cruise, my body shaking in confusion. Stopping at the top of my street, I cracked a smile. I was happy I wasn't going to jail that day.

Sometimes you knew the outcome and still kept rolling the dice, even after close calls. I was no Top Boy. I was not out there in the field with the full-timers serving on the corner. I was a Grade 5 kid trying to get some money on the side as a part-time runner. Many times, the people around me took risks to provide for their families—pushing dime bags or powder for baby formula—even if we were one to two decisions away from losing it all. On the corner, we rolled the dice on our future, the debt collection agency spammed our voicemails, and the adults overflowed the trash can with losing lottery tickets. Our financial future was up to chance. There had to be another way.

With the drop complete I got my money from Dre, which I used to buy oven-ready lasagna, mangoes, plantains, ramen noodles, and 99 cent cans of Allen's apple juice from the No Frills later that evening. I wasn't sure when or if I would go back out there to do drops again, but until then I had to get back to the stuff elementary children were supposed to do, like boring and robotic homework worksheets.

On my block, the people who made the most money hustling got the most respect. If you were broke or looked broke, you got dissed.

This started to become my norm, observing the business of street corner hustlers at different trap houses. From the outside it appeared to be fun. Profit, money, pay no taxes, new cars and clothes, eating foods with names we couldn't pronounce at restaurants on a regular basis, all-inclusive vacations, video games, and making music as you count it all up and restock your inventory. Early mornings, late nights, and celebrations every time we elevated the sales. When dope fiends got their cheques, the dealer's phone wouldn't stop ringing until their money ran out. At the time it seemed like the life to live. Trapping in all seasons. Parkas and Timberland boots. North Pole Hustlers. *I knew the business on the corner wasn't legal, but I knew if someone considered the transferable skills we all had, things would be different. If we had a different platform, a positive outlet, maybe we wouldn't have to work the streets.*

We didn't have the perks of living in wealthy communities, with their ecosystems of healthy grocery stores and farmer's markets, big budgets for school and community programs, financial education programs, science, technology, engineering, and mathematics centres, private schools, academic tutors, hockey, golf, tennis, arts and music programs for kids, start-up and entrepreneurial programs, doctor offices, dentists, law offices, real estate offices, well-maintained city parks, fitness centres, mental health services, clinics, banks, life insurance offices, reliable public transit, nicely paved roads. . . . All we had on our block was the rec centre that was vacant every couple years or so when city funding dried up, a couple of church programs, local community programs run by volunteers, broken concrete, potholed parking lots, and the people on the corner who were hustling to pass the time. In the world before smartphones, many around us still didn't have good WIFI or even a computer at home. The wealthy were set up to thrive. The richer neighbourhoods had generational wealth and we in the housing projects had generational trauma. We were left to survive.

> *Talent is universal. Opportunity is not.*
> —Rye Barcott

How could teachers say mathematics, science, and engineering weren't subjects for people who looked like me or came from my block?

In the words of Jay Morrison, "A drug dealer can only sell drugs, a true hustler can sell anything." I was 11 and science, mathematics, and engineering composed my entire being. It was my block experience—entrepreneurship, flipping things for cash. And I was just one of many talented people all around the block finding a way to hustle. I had the talent. We had the talent. They simply never gave us the platform to express our genius. Without being given an opportunity, we created our own on every street corner. I was young, but I already knew that there was a wedge between the world, the streets, and the school classroom. The haves, the have-nots, and everything else in between. There was talent in the hood; forward-thinking innovators and creative artists, architects, CEOs, directors, sales and marketing professionals, real estate agents, scientists, engineers, lawyers, doctors, bankers, investors, start-up owners, future technology experts, and more. We were solution-based thinkers. We had to be. The problem was how we used our intellectual gifts and energies and skills given our limited choices. The school system failed to give us a platform to share our transferable skills and experience "from the block."

Drug dealers sold drugs, but drug dealers who were hustlers were different. The hustlers juggled a lot of job titles—CEO, financial bookkeeper, marketing professional, product and inventory manager, and sales manager. Around here these were the people I looked up to. There was not much else because those who became successful in positive endeavours ultimately moved out and never came back. All we had were community centre staff who were rarely from the block and teachers who wouldn't dare set foot in the neighbourhood. Our parents were working multiple jobs, living paycheque to paycheque. Options for role models became limited. What I saw were drug runners and the hierarchy of people in the streets. Serve the curb and get a cut of the cash. We looked up to hustlers, but the real OGs were the ones who knew hustling was not the destination but a stepping stone to something else.

The deeper we go, the harder it is to get out. Soon the game is like an ocean; it's all we know, and we lose sight of how to get back to shore. We lose our childhood innocence because it's hard to get back to shore without assistance . . . without a village of support.

Hustling for quick cash meets a short-term need, but fast money is where the addiction begins. I have seen many get lost in the deep ocean of the game. First you start as a drug runner; you dip your toes in that ocean by doing drug drops. Then you go deeper, ankle- or knee-deep in the shallow end, a curb server. The unpredictable nature of the streets mimicked the riptides of the ocean—the powerful currents of water moving away from shore that can take even the strongest swimmer out to the middle of the ocean in a matter of seconds. From the shallow waters, those riptides could pull our entire bodies under water and take us deeper than we planned to go. You weren't safe unless you were on shore. Riptide deaths aren't caused by the tides of the streets. We often get too exhausted, struggling against the current to make it back to the shore. We run out of energy and stay out at sea. In the middle of the ocean—with no sight of shore—we are lost, so every direction we go in feels right.

But we can only tread water for so long before we stretch out our hand one last time, grabbing at the air we can no longer surface for. When the wave we do not see coming crashes down on our head, there is no more life. I saw this distance between the shore and the centre of the ocean as the trap.

In the streets, people never could stay on top forever. We were fighting external forces, our block, ourselves, and could be lined up by other blocks who sometimes sent girls to set up the mandem. At first, the streets embrace us, but eventually, when we get older, the concrete turns cold and it's no longer love . . . it's business. If a deal went south, the streets had no heart. People were taken for ransom. Ski masks or bare face, people came straight for the bag and families were caught in the middle. From the sandbox to the grave, but sometimes friends become enemies when money gets involved. *How do we get out of the current when no one showed us how?*

I feel like the system set us up. It felt like a twisted game of monopoly that came with old rules and no questions: school to prison to death. The pipeline. We'd inherited a system and a culture we had no part in creating. As kids, we were told things don't change, that's how it is—don't ask why, just find your place within it. In the classroom, teachers and guidance counsellors sentenced us to a slow, painful death. Across the city and the country, we low-income, Black, Indigenous, and brown kids were intentionally put into courses below our ability (including funnelling us into behavioural and special education classes). They offered zero support for our communities or our cultures, no educational support when we needed help, and they suspended and expelled us at disproportionate rates, sometimes, it seemed, just for breathing. The take home message seemed to be "we'll put up with you now, but after 18 you are on your own."

In the streets, we were faced with a fast death. We could be robbed, shot, arrested, jailed, or turned into a memory, depending on the day. Block beef was inherited. When things popped off, curb servers became street soldiers, fighting a street war we had no part in creating. Some beef was so deep we didn't even know why we were fighting to begin with; the beef started before we were even born. These streets had higher stakes, but the goal for all the legal and illegal hustlers remained the same: survive, by any means. Survive until we have the ability, one day, to find a way to get out of survival mode, and move on, finally, to thriving.

How do we move when both the street and the school classrooms chain our feet? How do we find our place within systems that imprison rather than free us?

As kids, we spent most of our time in places and spaces that made us feel like a somebody, places that made us feel smart, gave us purpose, and showed us love. If we didn't get it from school, extracurriculars, or non-existent community programs, we had to get it from the streets. The streets were the place that made us, at the time, feel valued and gave us a sense of purpose. As other outlets closed their doors on us, as our parents were busy juggling several jobs, the homies were all we had.

After a while, we started to embrace the streets that hugged us in our time of need. We hugged the block. We'd do anything to protect it. Though the government birthed and raised and sculpted the block into what it is today, some of us were prepared to die for it. We hugged the rented infrastructure. We don't own it; *they* do. And yet we die and hurt each other protecting what they built, protecting the conditions that were created to keep us from thriving.

Given this reality, we worked in the streets with what we were given. We had our own areas for business and, if we wanted to expand our operations into areas that weren't ours, we knew there would be problems.

From my own schooling experience, in the corner classroom I called home, neighbourhood to neighbourhood, we were products of the same struggle and the same hustle.

There was context for everything.

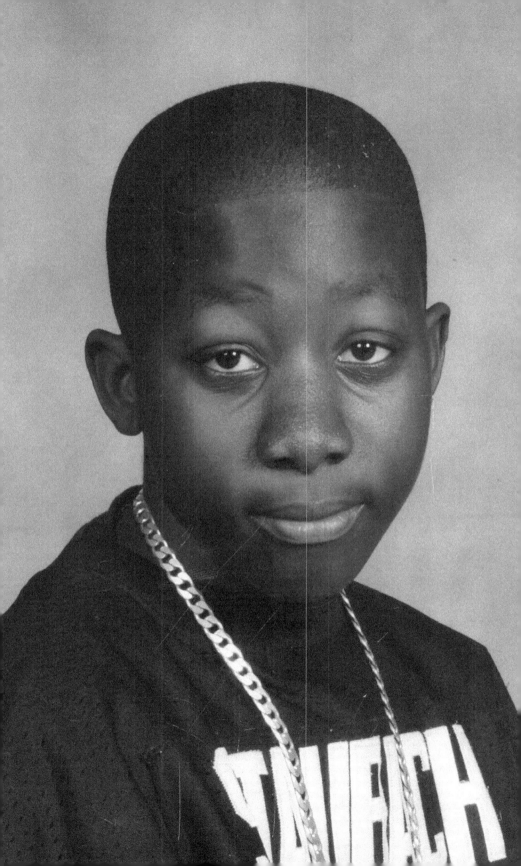

Cold Summers

Age 13: As I arrive on the corner, I pray I don't see a white sheet. I pray whoever got hit is still breathing.

By the time we arrived, the trees were wrapped in yellow tape and the streets were decorated in pulsing red and blue lights. Children, fathers, mothers, youth, and grandparents flooded the streets to see what happened. Watching the front of the crowd, I could see tears rippling down the faces of some people I knew from Southside. Many were wiping away the snot overflowing from their noses. I was frozen in the back of the crowd making sure my tears didn't drip down, especially in public. I had to wait until I was alone. This wasn't the first time and it wouldn't be the last.

Minutes before, a car pulled up. The clip was emptied. Metal flew through the air, cutting everything in its path. The metal ripped his skin apart as his blood dotted the sidewalk. Taking C out of his shoes. He slowly stumbled to the ground, catching his balance with enough energy to push the little girl out of the way of the fireworks that would take him to the turf. Stumbling to find his balance, one last moment, a final stand before the pavement embraced his body. The blood filled the cracks and broken crevices on the sidewalk. Six bullets to the chest, the flesh around his wounds were unrecognizable. There was a roller coaster of screams and shouts but no witnesses . . . just shells that dribbled across the sidewalk.

These were the modern-day heroes that didn't make the news. It was clear to the youngins that straight As in school couldn't stop stray bullets. This was not a DC or Marvel universe. This was the streets. These were the trenches. Wounded from the direct fire, he saved the girl when he could no longer save himself. When bullets sprayed, they began ripping everything in their path. Family. Community. Relationships. Bone and all. Even on summer nights, the concrete would turn cold. The heat that lit up the concrete wasn't solar but metal. In the summers, when it got hot, the grim reaper would come with open arms—death was in the air. We could smell it some days when we jumped off the porch. Whether adult, parent, or child, we stayed alert, some days with our head on a swivel. This was how we stayed alive, or at least how we would outrun the metal as it blew by our bodies . . . a near miss. Death didn't care how old we were, so we made sure we kept our head on a swivel with a balanced sense of paranoia. Sometimes I replay this shooting in my head on repeat. What if I didn't turn around to go back inside my house to grab food before going to the ball court? I would have been right there where it went down.

The ambulance took him. No white sheets. No chalk.

I was hoping that he would make it. I didn't want to see anymore murals or hashtags. No faces on T-shirts. We just wanted to see C smile again. With my thoughts racing a mile a minute, I couldn't remember everything that happened after the paramedics came. What I do remember is not sleeping that night. I remember being lost and without direction. We couldn't lose another community leader who had done so much to bring hope to the block.

After the first of six bullets hit, I thought of his mother staring at the wall for the next few years. I thought of brothers and sisters imprisoned in their own neighbourhood because they were too scared to come outside. I thought of the metal ripping the flesh of the community, leaving everyone on the block squirming from a kind of emotional pain we didn't know how to express. I thought of the curb servers chained to trenches we didn't create. I thought of the inspiration C brought to us by showing us there was another way to live; that selling rocks wasn't the only way to make it. When the sixth bullet hit his chest and he stumbled to the ground, I thought of Blue Boy, stolen from us two years prior. Wrong place. Wrong time. We weren't prepared to lose another.

The next day, I heard from the grandmas on the block that our community leader C was stable and waiting to wake up. So we waited and continued to pray. Even though we knew these things would happen again. The block was happy to see him pull through, but the emotional toll on the community would be felt for too many years to count.

C was alive, but we still had the mourning ritual on the neighbourhood street corner for the ones who weren't as lucky as he was. Year after year, since I was kid, I learned the importance of pouring some before we drink some. It was a hood spiritual. Those we lost drank before we did. This was one way we kept their memory alive.

Years later, I would discover that what goes on in the streets is not so different from what goes down on the battlefield. In the military, people go through rigorous mental, physical, emotional, and psychological training year after year to prepare themselves for battle. More often than not, soldiers returning from their deployment on the frontlines of war come back sick with severe psychological distress. One of the most common diagnoses is post-traumatic stress disorder (PTSD). It is a societal norm to empathize with people in the military who have experienced extreme acts of violence, but there is no empathy for the modern warzone of the streets. In the streets, babies, children, youth, fathers, mothers, and grandparents have no rigorous training to prepare themselves for war, but they can find themselves in the midst of war at any time. These were the modern-day trenches.

In these trenches, gunfire could go down at any point: waiting at the bus stop to go to work, playing in the park at recess, enjoying backyard BBQs, walking home from the basketball court, walking to the mosque or church for religious activities, or even walking to get groceries. This all resulted in what I called neighbourhood PTSD, the kind born from poverty and the slew of traumas that come from the streets. Drugs, gun violence, stabbings, police killings, police brutality, wrongful arrests, police raids, homicides, robberies, suicides, abuse— too many things for a child to process. You can also add poverty, lack of affordable housing, underfunded schools and community programs, and no mental health support services.

Sometimes, when I closed my eyes at night as a child, I would hear gunshots, but when I opened them nothing had happened, it was all in my head. The yellow tape, pulsing sirens, and screams of pain became normal to our ears before we even had our two front teeth. Trauma from birth. Set up to die before we were born. Sooner or later we all lost touch with who we were before everyone around us started to disappear. It was a cold summer.

We grew up fast while the unmarked cars pulled up slow.

On any given day it felt like there was a war going on inside my head. We saw things that we shouldn't. We were too young. We just wanted to be kids.

Unfortunately, we didn't know how to name trauma because we normalized it. It wasn't until we stepped outside of it to get a bird's-eye view that we realized the stuff we saw in the streets was not normal and not everyone was living like this. Growing up, my ecosystem was simple: mainly stay in my hood and, if I ventured out, only travel to Savings Mart to get small groceries, Backwoods for the OGs, Scarborough Town Centre for fresh gear, the Bluffs and Lake Ontario, the Toronto Zoo, the Rouge River, the Cineplex movie theatre at Warden and Eglinton, and the Shoppers' World plaza on the Danforth. As kids, we never ventured out of the block, we never went to areas we weren't from, so my view throughout my childhood was limited. But once I got older, I noticed how much we were suffering in silence, how much we relied on one specific way to cope. I called it Serial Escapism.

Serial escapism was the routine process of reaching for a lifestyle or activity to temporarily escape from the reality of trauma and emotional pain. To numb or delay the pain from being felt. Liquor our kidneys. Smoke our lungs. Fill our veins. Snow our noses. All drugs, any drugs. I would also see excessive volunteerism or studying, house cleaning, fanaticism over sports and fitness, workaholics, and some who slid deeper into the street life of hustling. Anything to keep busy. To get our mind off things. Anything to provide us a sense of value, an outlet, or an experience that numbs the pain long enough that we didn't have to be alone with our own thoughts. Some escape vehicles were healthier than others, but many I saw were unhealthy. Yes, hurt people hurt people, but first, hurt people tend to hurt themselves, their health.

We were just self-medicating. Sometimes we needed to get high to get by.

We didn't talk about mental health, but I knew the mental health on the block was not good under the conditions we lived in. For a while, people said nothing. Drugs opened their arms to many of us when we couldn't deal with situations. Because we didn't know how. The bottle tapped us on the shoulder when all we wanted was the pain to go away. We never thought it would trap us. We didn't have mental health therapy so instead we rolled the fattest blunts in Backwoods Smokes. Puff puff pass.

I always wondered if escapism was the reason some of the university graduates and scholarship-level athletes from our hood did so well. I wondered if our grind and laser focus first started as a way to escape when things got really hard and continued when things kept happening, one after another, giving us no time to process. I thought we were living in hell, so we needed to find an outlet to get to heaven. This was serial escapism, a survival mechanism. We acted on instinct as a way to survive. By any means necessary. Finding something to hug us for the moment even if it couldn't heal us for the long-term.

We were reaching to escape when what we actually needed was someone to reach for us, to help us find a way towards healing and a way towards mental wellness instead of trying to outrun the pain ourselves. We could reach to numb the pain again, but eventually our past would outrun us. Years later, when I was older, the pain of what we experienced on the block would make sense. Some people who were without help turned to drugs as a way to cope and got severely addicted. Some people popped pills like Tic Tacs, or they shot up with needles in places I was taught never to play with bare feet. At the time, we called those people fiends, but the truth is that they were humans suffering from pain and trauma they didn't know how to treat. They were people first.

We are pressured to survive, doing what we can to provide for our loved ones with very little time to process what we see. I don't know how, but we find ways to recover the best we can with cookouts, block parties, soccer tournaments, arts and music festivals, freestyle hip hop battles, b-ball, Dominoes, cards, and even fun days for the kids. Anything that is about community and bringing people outside and together. We find a way to bounce back. We never really do, but we try. We do our best. In the end, we just want to live. I just want to live.

> *I believe that if we understood ourselves better, we would damage ourselves less.*
> —James Baldwin

I didn't have my escape plan yet, but I was looking for one. The serial escape outlets around me were not the best options so I had to be strategic and patient. I wish someone would have told us *it's okay to not be okay* and that we didn't have to suffer in silence. I wish someone would have told us that if we didn't heal our wounds, we would continue to bleed. If we did want to heal, we didn't even know where to start. The second we had a chance to begin healing from the trauma, something else would happen that we had to deal with. There was always some shit going down. I was only 13, but sometimes I wanted to run away and never come back.

We became endangered species under neighbourhood conditions we didn't create. Though people around me prayed, the conditions the city left us in seemed to block the prayers from being heard. The elements around us pressured us to make decisions we were not always proud of. We were never desensitized to pain, as the media liked to portray. Every block, every hood, every community member felt and knew the pain all too well. We couldn't run from it. It was bound to show up at some point or other.

As humans, we choose to surround ourselves with people who provide us a sense of community, a sense of purpose, and a sense of identity. If we couldn't find that sense of community and belonging at home, because our parents were busy working multiple jobs, and we couldn't find it at school, which was busy pushing us out, we would find community in the streets and the people we meet out there. This was my story and the story of those around me.

> *When children attend schools that place a greater value on discipline and security than on knowledge and intellectual development, they are attending prep schools for prison.*
> —Angela Davis

The worst form of violence is racism and poverty. It killed us quick or slow until it left us without air.

If violence or crime happened on our side of town, we were always the easy targets to blame. Meanwhile, the politicians and those in positions of power went unpunished. Some teachers are too scared to get to the root of the problem, to keep the educational policy makers accountable for their actions—for creating the conditions for this stuff to happen. And of course, they live far enough away that they don't have to deal with it when sparks fly. The second they sign the dotted line they are enacting a form of violence on many of us across the city and country . . . an education system, from Kindergarten to Grade 12, that streams us low-income and Black kids into courses below our ability, limiting our future opportunities before we even learn to read and write. Political authorities need to be held accountable for their silence. Politicians and the education system are responsible for creating the conditions that allow the pain to happen.

When community members are murdered in the neighbourhoods of political authorities, they say, "They did not deserve it." When we die, their hearts do not move. They say nothing. Their inaction communicates their belief that our communities somehow deserve it. We aren't afforded the same human response to loss and pain because to them we aren't human. This made my blood boil because they snitched on themselves. To me, the city feels like a graveyard filled with landmines. Run by people who show up for photo ops and handshakes, people who are all too happy to sign death into legislation and create the conditions that force people to survive by any means.

It's hard to learn when you feel hungry, silenced, incarcerated; when you are dealing with untreated PTSD. Wounded from the bodies that spread out on the pavement. Our souls carry the burden of everything before we carry our first book bag to grade school. As a child, all I wanted was to see the sun shining tomorrow. I wish someone would have told me "trauma is not your fault and some of it is generational, passed down." All of this made it hard to be present and successful in a school that felt like a prison, another form of trauma. To me, a real educational space embraces curiosity and makes us feel safe to be ourselves. Unfortunately, the closest I could get wasn't school but the local Black barbershop. School was more focused on compliance. I felt they were preparing us for jail rather than preparing us to live a good life. The failure of many schools in the hood is that too many teachers focus on enforcing the law, acting like prison guards. Instead, we need teachers who are gardeners, people who create environments for us to grow. Much of Canada, like the US, loves Black culture and Black contributions to society, but they remain silent when we fight for justice and basic human rights. The conclusion: they love Black culture, but they don't love Black people.

Police didn't protect our hoods. And as our homies and family members across the city died, many before the age of 25, I started to see why some people felt the pressure to be strapped for protection. No one I knew wanted gun violence . . . not even the dealers. With the block hot and the police now patrolling, that was bad for business. Sales and cash would come in slower and little mouths needed to be fed.

I was young but I noticed the streets ran by different rules. In the streets, some things were done on sight. In some cases it was either you or them. I didn't support it, but I started to understand the importance of being aware of my surroundings, especially when beef was in the air.

The mainstream news called 2005 the "year of the gun." They would say the same thing about 2018, when the police were over-funded and found their budget increased again (while every and all community resources and opportunities were defunded). While the pockets of corporations and the police system got fatter, low-income communities were receiving bread crumbs. This was Toronto.

In the streets, there are no winners. No one stays on top forever. At some point we all lose. Whether it's eulogies, prison visitations, hospital ER visits, staring down the barrel of a gun, or being handcuffed and thrown into the back of the cruiser, death comes like a rerun.

When things popped off, we just had to try and make it through the night.

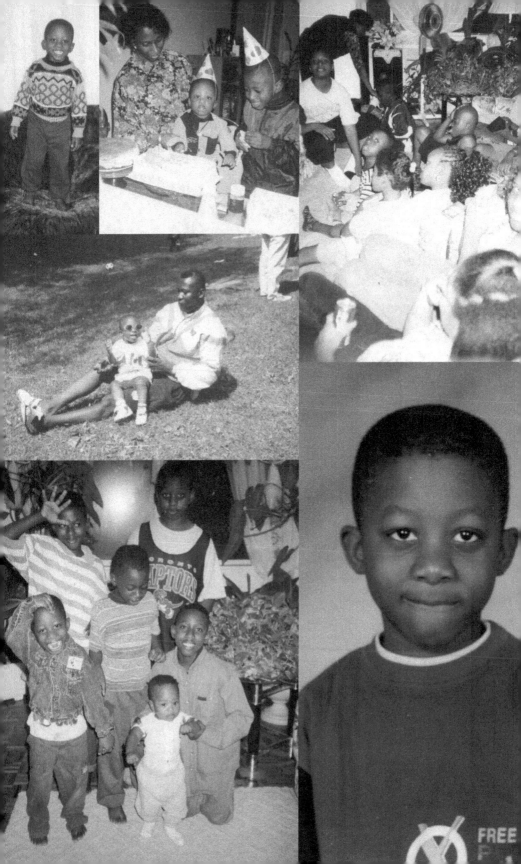

The Prairies

Location: *Caronport, Saskatchewan (4173 km from Halifax)*
7:30 a.m.: *Eastbound to Africville, Halifax, Nova Scotia*

I was back in the middle of the Prairies once again. It was
enjoyable enough to drive through farm fields and country-
side, but biking through it seemed like a bad idea.

Today, we woke up earlier than usual so I could get ready to cycle
130 km to another small town we had never heard of. The green fields
were so vibrant and fresh that it looked untouched by humans. I was
seeing the kind of green that I had once only found in movies. With
endless flat lands, hundreds of kilometres of long country roads, tractors on farm land, and cows mooing all day, every day, I was way too
far from my hood in Scarborough. I had seen more cows than people
over those past two weeks, and I swear there was only one washroom
every 200 km and it was in a gas station. Just gazing at the open field
from the back seat of the van made me want to run through the acres
of grass and lay in the middle of the land and take a nap for the rest of
the summer.

Chilling on the shoulder of the Trans-Canada Highway, we looked
out at what felt like the flattest place on the planet; where you can
cycle for 20 km and feel like you didn't move at all. Biking felt like I
was staring at a blank wall that never changed. I can't remember ever
looking up from the bike. I just kept my head down, trying to get back

to Ontario as fast as physically possible. Usually the Prairies was an easier ride. Compared to the mountains, there was a lower elevation and no headwinds, but this time it was different. The day prior, the crosswinds turned into headwinds. I was battling Mother Nature to stay balanced on my thin bike wheels. It was my hope that the wind would let up and I could pick up some speed. I just wanted to get back to Toronto. I needed some homecooked and well-seasoned Caribbean and African food from each corner of the continent. In most small town restaurants and diners I was getting the exact opposite of what I was used to . . . food without seasoning.

My body was hanging on by a thread. But I kept it a secret. I didn't want the crew to worry about me. I would wake up every day feeling like I didn't sleep. It wasn't the ride that made it difficult but everything on top of it. Riding all day, speaking at venues at night, managing the team and the injuries I was getting along the way. I could no longer feel my hamstrings. I hobbled up and down the stairs at the end of most days as walking became its own chore. My shoulders and trap muscles would start contracting involuntarily and the knots in my back would send a shooting pain down my spine every hour. Since road bikes have no shocks, my body absorbed all the repetitive vibrations of the road. Somedays I was left with no choice but to cycle with one arm because my neck muscles didn't have the energy to hold my head up. With one arm I could at least give my body and neck a break from the vibrations until my muscles stopped acting up. On the outside, I looked good. On the inside, I knew why my feet were staining my shoes red. My toes were un-recognizable. My feet were sweating buckets. I hadn't cut my nails in two weeks and they would just give up on me and fall off in my cycling shoes. Whoever said "if it doesn't kill you, it makes you stronger" was lying.

Sitting on the back of the trailer, I peeked around the car and looked up at Cameron in the driver seat scratching his head. He was usually calm, cool, and collected so I knew something was up. I knew we were in trouble if the driver, the only driver, was screwing up his face. I quickly realized the car wasn't starting. I had never told the team . . . but we had no emergency plans for mechanical issues. We needed to think fast. Raising the hood, Cameron started doing things the average driver with zero mechanic understanding, like me, would understand. I just took a walk up the shoulder of the highway for some fresh air and left it for the crew to figure out without me.

We were nowhere close to finishing the ride but I was tired of going through small towns across Canada. I was ready to go home to chill with the fam.

Many Canadians I met along the way didn't realize racism is embedded in our country just like it is in the United States. The only difference was that Canada was trying to hide it at all costs, pointing fingers south of the border instead of dealing with the issues head on in our own country. Every night, in each new city, our hosts were welcoming, but the small towns across the country made me feel like I was in Jordan Peele's horror movie *Get Out*. If someone were to ask me how it feels to cycle across Canada, I would point them to the movie. Cycling across Canada, I saw some of the most beautiful scenery I have ever seen in my life and was reminded of every movie where the Black person dies first. From confederate flags, Make America Great Again hats, and lawn gnomes on the porches of white family homes that depicted racist visuals of African slaves and Indigenous peoples facing genocide, Canada was no different than the countries they tried to distance themselves from. In many ways, Canada and the US are one and the same. We are two arms of the same beast. Many people are living with their eyes closed. I quickly noticed that many of the people I met in each new town or city didn't even know there was an Indigenous reserve right next door to where they had lived for decades. It was clear to me that people stay in their bubbles and create false ideas and damaging stereotypes about people who live outside their bubbles. In many ways, they create a life in which Indigenous and Black people don't exist.

Canada is segregated as a country, even within its most diverse cities like Toronto. A simple online investigation makes it clear that it's segregated by race and class.

We were almost halfway through Canada, but I was cycling alone. Back in the mountains of Western Canada, Addisiane's knees had become so swollen that the doc at the hospital said he needed a week or two off of cycling to regain the mobility he had lost in his joints. He was now the team manager, ensuring we were on schedule and fuelled with food and water, and that the bike chains were clean of debris and lubed so I could ride efficiently every day. Since the mountains, I had been cycling all day every day with only the cows screaming in the distance. I didn't know when he would be back, but I had to carry the weight until then.

Cameron was on pace to become our team hero if he figured out how to start the car. Turns out he was perfect for the job.

I didn't know Cameron before Ride for Promise. I met him the day we left Toronto to drive to Vancouver. He was only 19, born and raised in a small town of only 4000 people in Norwood, just east of Peterborough, Ontario. Another predominantly white township neighbouring Addisiane's hometown of Havelock. Standing 6 foot 7 inches, he was a giant, but he was soft hearted and a great BBQ chef. Anytime we stopped on the side of the road to cook a meal, he hooked it up. He was friends with Addisiane. They met working security at a nightclub and have been homies ever since. We needed a driver for our support van, and Addisiane persuaded him to help out, winning him over with the added bonus of seeing Canada for free thanks to the sponsors who made the trip possible. Between cycling and late-night conversations with drinks under the stars, I found out he comes from a family of mechanics and also races cars on dirt tracks across Canada, where he's won numerous races on major platforms. I don't remember the names, but knowing how humble he was, I knew he was doing it bigger than he was making it seem.

Cameron was the only person who was capable of fixing the issue that could derail our trip. We had a tight schedule, and we couldn't afford to miss one day all summer. We had dinners and speaking events lined up in each city every night, and if we were late, we wouldn't have a place to speak, eat, or even sleep. Sleeping in the car or tent was not an option. I made a commitment to give my team, especially Jarrett, a good bed to sleep in each night even though I was the only one who actually needed good sleep because if I didn't, I wouldn't be able to ride or speak.

Jarrett was our crew's secret MVP. He was mostly behind the scenes, taking photos and filming anything he could from the ride, including the bloopers. He was born and raised in Cornwall, a small town outside of Ottawa, Ontario. We met for the first time two months before the ride when I was studying in Sao Paulo, Brazil, with other Brazilian teachers, professors, activists, and freelance journalists. Jarrett was filming the trip to make a mini documentary for the Ontario Tech University, but during the late hours we would meet in the hotel lobby and chop it up, crack jokes, and have solid conversations about activism. Though he wasn't from the city, he was the kind of person who could be anywhere, amongst people with different experiences, backgrounds, or hobbies and always hold his own and be himself. He was the chillest person and the only skater I knew. To me, he was our Tony Hawk.

Staring into the distance on the Trans-Canada Highway, I started to see the light rays bend on the road, creating shimmers of heat that were vibrating in front of me. It created the illusion that light was reflecting off a pool of water in the middle of the street ahead. It was 35+ degrees Celsius that day but my mind was drifting off into dreamland. As my eyelids began to flutter, I began losing touch with the reality of where I was and what I was doing in the present. My mind started to drift back to the heat wave I experienced when I was 13. To the time my house was on fire.

I felt like I was still asleep, dreaming. I slowly opened my eyes, glancing at the clock: 2:43 a.m. My eyes wandered slightly left, towards the light that I thought was the sun. The dancing glow of orange and bright yellow in the otherwise dark room made me screw up my face. I thought I was in a black hole orbiting the sun with my clock radio in hand. Moving my head on a swivel, I glanced to the right and saw the shadowy outline of what looked like a person. Then a pair of hands wrapped around my shoulders. A hold of love and fear. With no audio registering in my brain, the vast blackness disappeared and the brightness of the sun behind me illuminated my mother's face.

Droplets formed in the corner of her eyes just waiting to drip down. The moisture along her hair line made her face shiny as the heat trickled down her cheek to her chin. I could sense that danger was near. Snapping out of my sleep hypnosis, I heard my neighbour screaming and the echoes of fists smashing on the kitchen windows. I was in my room. I was not dreaming.

A thick fog invaded my nostrils as my body was shaken awake. The smoke was near, reducing visibility and steaming up all the windows, making it impossible to see outside. I was up in a matter of seconds after hearing my mom cry out my name.

Throwing the blanket off my legs, I jumped off the bed, opened my bedroom door, and ran down the two flights of stairs with my mom leading the way. We double checked that no one was in the kitchen, basement, and other bedrooms to make sure everyone else was out. Then we made our way out the back door, slamming it behind us. We stood outside, watching the front porch of my house crackling and cooking in the flames. It was a 30 foot bonfire without the smores kit. The house was literally lit.

The fire truck was screaming in the distance and the closer it got to us, the louder I could hear my heart and mom's pulse exploding in my ear. She pulled me in and squeezed me tight like I was the only thing she had left. Running her fingers through my mini afro, she said, "Everything is going to be alright," but this time with a crackle in her voice that I had never heard before. I was no longer confident that things would be alright. I didn't know what to believe anymore. I was still trying to figure out why my house was on fire.

Suddenly, the image of my house fire starts to blur and I'm back on the country road in the Prairies. I only left the present moment for three seconds but to me it felt like a movie.

Outside the gas station, I can hear the news coming from a nearby transport truck. They were talking about the forest fires that were still actively spreading in British Columbia. I stared at Cameron, Addisiane, and Jarrett across the road in the only mechanic shop in this small town of Caronport, where we had just stayed the night. With a population of 1000, it had a Bible college, a gas station, and coincidentally, a mechanic shop that opened for business at the same time the van failed to start.

By the time I walked back to the crew, the car had received a couple jolts of electricity to get it going. Addisiane grabbed my bike out of the van, flipped it over, and pedalled 20 rotations to examine the chain debris and cleanliness. With a wet towel covered in chain cleaner, he wrapped the chain and pedalled for 20 more rotations to wipe the chain and make sure it was clean of all the dirt, debris, and grime. To finish the job, he grabbed the bike lube and dripped it between each chain link. With the chain clean, cycling would be a lot more efficient and the bike would remain in good health. Now I was on my way to start my 130 km cycling day. It was an hour later than I wanted, but we were happy the trip was not over.

I loaded up my pockets with skittles, fuzzy peaches, Gatorade, coconut water, three bananas, and chocolate chip cookies from the night before. For good luck, I wrapped a couple slices of cold Costco pizza in brown napkins and put them in the back pockets of my cycling jersey. With the heat doing its magic, I knew I would have oven-ready pizza a couple hours into the ride. At first, I was eating healthy food to refuel my body and give long-term energy to my muscles, but that quickly switched to junk food. I was burning so many calories and eating 20 plus times per day so I got bored and had to switch it up.

As an adult, I had an easier time accepting and looking for help from others, but I wasn't always like this. Eventually I learned the importance of having mentors and helpers in your life. From the house fire days, I realized I couldn't go through life alone. Some people came into my life for a reason and some for a season. Without them, I wouldn't have overcome the barriers I faced along the way. Sometimes help was just around the corner. I just had to be patient, take a deep breath, and look around to see who is who and what is what. I had to be present, otherwise I would miss who the real ones were. Today my helpers along the way were Addisiane, Cameron, and Jarrett, but when I was younger it was my mom and my homie Dre.

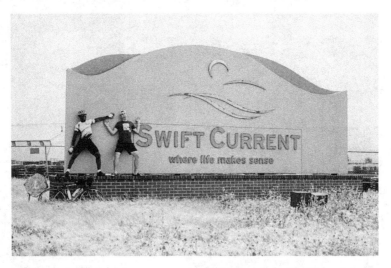

Dre

*The opposite of poverty is not wealth; the opposite
of poverty is justice.*

—Bryan Stevenson

Age 14: I held the handle of the phone that was attached
to the wall and stared into his eyes before putting it to
my ear to talk. Sitting on the other side of the bulletproof glass was my
friend's brother, Dre. The same Dre who taught me the ropes of the
streets. He was now in prison.

Entering the building felt like *déjà vu*. My mind sprinted for answers. This building looked, sounded, and smelled the same as public
school. Similarly, people were treated like animals, despite being full
human beings. The prison guards walking the halls reminded me of
the hall monitors and cops that patrolled the schoolyard.

Putting the phone to my ear, I hesitated again. Then I froze, temporarily forgetting how to talk or even how to hold a phone, as if I
never had before. I can't really remember the first words I said. I think
I asked if he was okay. Dre probably said he was good, but I knew he
was lying. It was written all over his face. I knew what survival and
keeping it together looked like when I saw it. I don't remember saying
anything at all. He was directly in front of me yet he seemed light-
years away. I would have embraced him if only the mile-thick window
wasn't in the way. I don't remember the last time I formed a tear but

today I knew I very well could. Fourteen years of holding it in to be "strong"—as though strength was about forgetting how to feel and how to show love.

Dre taught me about life in the streets and in prison. Though he dropped out of high school, I noticed that teachers often felt threatened by his intelligence. I knew he was caught up in the street life but if anyone talked to him long enough they would realize he was smart and creative. At the end of the day, none of that was important anymore because he was no longer with us on the outside.

Before this country was named Canada, Indigenous communities were here coast to coast, taking care of the land and people with their own politically and socially advanced nations. These communities had expert knowledge and wisdom in every area from architecture and mathematics to technology, planting and irrigation, astronomy, writing, agriculture, physics, science, medicine, engineering, mining, geology and more. When Europeans arrived, they quickly turned it into a warzone, and had the audacity to label their actions "discovery." From the slavery and genocide of Indigenous and African peoples on this land to mass incarceration of poor, Indigenous, Black, and brown people, this was always the plan for colonization. To the OGs on the block like Dre, slavery was not abolished but reformed. Same game, different name.

Once I started asking questions, it was Dre—a high school dropout, drug dealer, and now inmate—who gave me some answers, who helped me understand what I was seeing in our community, and what we were experiencing. This was when I began to see Dre's relationship with books and how books (that I was too young to read then) were changing how he saw our collective situation living on the block.

He told me about how he hated reading because the books available to him at school were boring and a waste of his time. But once in prison, he found books that interested him and helped him see his life and the block differently. He believed there had to be another way, something other than what was given to us. I could tell there was a glow and something about him that wasn't there before he went inside. He said Africa did not need the world, but the world needed Africa.

Dre also told me stories of how he spent days, weeks, and months sitting in solitary confinement doing 23 plus 1—23 hours of darkness and, if you were lucky, one hour of sunshine. Things weren't looking great for him. He was caught hustling to pay his family's rent, which was two months late.

Even though I didn't know the charges, Dre kept the faith that he would get out soon, but from what I heard on the outside, he wasn't coming home for a long time and hadn't yet faced the facts.

I remember seeing his heavy heart in his eyes.

The same people who were supposed to be Dre's friends didn't visit him, drop money in his canteen, or even call him. With them it was only ever about the money. Since he was no longer of any use to them behind bars, they left him. Our relationship was different because it was never about the money. Dre reminded me to use the skills I learned from the streets to do more positive things and get legit. I didn't know what that meant at 14, but what he told me made me want to be something different than what I was seeing around me. He said I reminded him of a younger version of himself. I knew it was the entrepreneur in me. He taught me that the street corner was not the destination, it was a stop on the road. It was a road I was now officially leaving, but it would take time since I didn't know where to start.

At the time, I didn't know what he meant, but in a matter of seconds, right as we were getting into the meat of the conversation, our visit was over. Sirens started to scream and red and white lights started pulsing. The guards flooded the room, swiftly ending all conversations. All the people who were incarcerated, including Dre, disappeared like ghosts. Frozen, I don't remember what followed. If our time hadn't been cut short by the lockdown he would have told me what books he was reading before he was shipped away.

I didn't know it at that time, but this would be the last time I would see him for 13 years; they shipped him too far away for my pocket change to reach. Only phone calls were possible.

This was the day I learned of the three places that felt like prison to me. Places that we didn't create but had to learn to live with: the streets, school, and prison.

As a child, I thought prison was supposed to ensure that you came out better than when you went in. But, in many ways, everyone I knew came out more damaged mentally, spiritually, emotionally, and physically. There were no free programs for transitioning back to society, no rehab, no mental health services, or education programs. The transition was so difficult that I watched a lot of my friends just disappear after they got released. They either went back to jail, got sucked back into the streets, or relocated to different cities just to survive and get a fresh start.

> *I am a human being. Nothing human can be alien to me.*
> —Maya Angelou

Dre was my inspiration, my starting point. I had to figure out what books he was reading because he was moving differently. I wanted to get on his wave and try it out.

I never liked reading books, at least not the ones given to us in school. The majority of the books on the classroom bookshelf were written by white men and women. I wasn't interested in the so-called classics the so-called teachers enjoyed decades before I was born. To me, those classics were forced upon us. Clearly the world I lived in was not represented in these books, and across genres, the worlds they described weren't of much interest to me. The stories were so limited in perspective, so narrow in view. I was interested in books that were reflective of the world, my time, and my cuture. Books by Black authors or anyone who was not white. These books were rare to find in school but when we got our hands on them, they were *lit*. Even the white homies were in love with books written by authors of colour . . . they knew the vibe. It wasn't simply the author's skin colour that made them amazing authors, but the experiences they shared. It was the storytelling tradition they came from, their ability to paint pictures and movies with words. They wrote about all-encompassing worlds in sci-fi, fiction, nonfiction, history, and more.

One day, I watched an interview with Baltimore city author D. Watkins, which I had stumbled upon on YouTube. He highly recommended *The Coldest Winter Ever* by Sister Souljah, so I decided to pick it up. It was one of the best decisions I ever made. This book would become one of my favourite novels of all time. Written in the urban fiction genre, this book resonated deeply with me and gave me a new perspective on communities like mine. I didn't know what happened in the streets could be in books. Not only could they be written about, they could become bestsellers. I was cheesed that I hadn't read books like this in school. It wasn't until I was in my 20s that I found the books I had always wanted as a kid but couldn't get in school. On the block, we were used to limited choices and limited opportunities, with no real freedom to choose what we could read. This always bothered me but it also was the norm.

> *Drugs rob every person, man, woman, and child of their beauty. Drugs turn people into animals who can only respond to instincts. Drugs are so powerful they eradicate the God in both the taker and the giver.*
>
> —Sister Souljah

I began to notice that drugs came in many forms in my community, and I'm not just referring to the ones you find in the streets. Politicians addicted to power were used to habitually destroying communities. These people needed help. They were twisted.

As a kid, I noticed the people who were addicted to drugs couldn't go cold turkey or they would die. Sometimes the dealers, if they could, would help them get clean slowly, especially if it was a friend's family member who was secretly buying without them knowing. They weren't doctors and often got it wrong, but they tried reducing doses little by little. This wasn't street code for how it was typically supposed to go down, but out on the corner they were still human. The dealers would eventually lose money and a customer but if they could take the financial hit and bounce back, they would. Rehab clinics and doctors didn't exist in our area so sometimes the dealer tried to be the healer.

In most cases, in my community, we were stuck in the middle if we really needed the money to provide for our family. Though the rock we were selling was slowly destroying families in our community, we had limited choices to make money. So we decided to sell it anyways.

No human chooses this life from their first breath of existence. There is a context for everything. No one is born longing to mess up their life . . . absolutely no one. Being Black in Canada was no different than it was for my cousins across the United States who spoke of similar realities. It was the same game, just a different location. All we had to do was keep our heads above water long enough to make something of our lives.

> *And it is that one percent, the heads of large corporations, who control the policies of the news media and determine what you and I hear on the radio, read in the newspapers, and see on television. It is more important for us to think about where the media gets its information.*
>
> —Assata Shakur

Each time someone goes to prison, I notice that politicians and the mainstream news like to wash their hands clean as if they've solved "the problem." I notice how they never discuss the social injustices that cause the issues we see—the conditions of poverty that are the foundation for most violence, drug-related crime, and poor outcomes in school.

I notice that when society fails to address root causes it's us on the block who are left to receive the blame for society's problems. But we didn't design these streets. We did not underfund public schools and community programs. We were not responsible for denying funds to mental health and addiction services, affordable housing, education, employment and social services, services for the homeless, community services, health care, and afterschool programs. We were children born to live, but under the conditions they created for us, the message was clear: they believed we were born to die.

It's clear there is not one answer to solve all the issues, but I knew what the politicians were doing wasn't working. *Mainly, they were framing poverty as a personal problem rather than a systemic failure and structural design.*

As a child I always heard people talk about the crabs in the barrel pulling each other down as one gets close to the top, but how come no one ever asked who built the barrel and put the crabs in it to begin with?

The streets and the system that put us in the housing projects felt similar. They use self-hate as a business strategy. Befriend us. Use us for their benefit. Exploit us. Mislead us. Push us to the edge. Then, when they are done with us, they get rid of us because we are no longer needed. And like any hood, regardless of pigment, horizontal violence occurs; we hurt each other. Then the system washes its hands clean. Rinse, wash, repeat. Self-hate is a business strategy and we weren't the ones making profit. They call it a business. I call it a trap.

As a child in a house of silence, what are we supposed to do if we have to be our own mother and father? What if it is easier to do what we see than create a new reality for ourselves? If we were able to expose ourselves to different experiences, people, and opportunities instead of what we typically see around us, we could also learn new things and envision a new type of life for ourselves.

I knew that what we consistently saw around us is what we would likely become.

> *a system*
> *that plants children in soil*
> *riddled with weeds*
> *and then uproots them for not flourishing.*
> *-mass incarceration*
> —Ogorchukwu

Mama Dukes

There is no such thing as a single-issue struggle because we do not live single-issue lives.

—Audre Lorde

ge 14: I never liked the rain because when it rained, it poured. The hard pill to swallow was dealing with the aftermath of the mud. The aftereffects of the raindrops dribbled across the uneven pavement and cut through the ceiling tiles onto the living room floor.

My mind was playing tricks on me. I started to see the reaper coming for me in my nightmares. Trauma came for me in my sleep, with scenes as real as the bed I was lying in. Throughout my life, I've had dreams of bleeding out. The past had a hold on me, so I had a hard time being present. I had many experiences I knew I would never share, and the ones I could would be the superficial ones. Some stories were never meant to be shared more than once. From time to time, I would be lucky enough to be present and at peace, but it was only around two things: my mom and our hood farm.

I had a hood garden. A backyard garden with baby tomatoes, carrots, spaghetti squash, romaine lettuce, baby red peppers, green onions, and other greens for homemade Guyanese pepper sauce. My dad gave us all a passion for bikes and a love for gardens. He was always working multiple jobs, I never knew where, but in his absence the garden fathered us. My older brothers were always out and didn't pay much mind to the farm, but my mom and I bonded as we took care of the garden together when she was home.

Nothing compares to growing your own food, from watering the garden and tending the soil to chasing away the raccoons and squirrels. I felt like this backyard was mine. I wondered what we could grow if we had more space, like those acre-long fields we saw on TV. I loved the city and will forever be a city kid, but having some land of my own has always been a dream.

Reminiscing on grade school days, I remember sitting on my mom's lap, watching the garden and just being still with nature. The caterpillars always fascinated me, although it's the butterfly that many people worship. Caterpillars were the beauty that I needed every day. It seemed to me that the caterpillar should be praised for what it was capable of becoming after it had to crawl through the mud for the first phase of its life. As a child, I always wanted to know if the caterpillar knew it was destined to be a butterfly before it was protected by the cocoon. The caterpillar and I were a lot alike. I didn't have a cocoon, but the closest I could get to feeling protected and safe was in the presence of my mom. Eventually I'd learned to appreciate the butterfly more as I learned what the caterpillar had gone through to become one.

⬧⬧⬧⬧⬧

This light in my life came to a dim close as we moved from the three-bedroom, two-storey house to a two-bedroom apartment at the back of the block with five people and no garden. As always, we would find a way to make it work even if we could hear the roaches crawling through the ceiling on our first night sleeping in the new apartment.

I was only two months away from starting high school as a freshman. I was sleeping on the couch. With five people, there was minimal space in the tiny two-bedroom apartment. The plan was to be here from Grades 9 to 12. We had a clean apartment, but because we were in an older building, we inherited the bugs as well as the tenants. We had to deal with roaches and resurgent cases of bed bugs that made it impossible to sleep as our skin would be eaten alive. Since then, shared laundry rooms always give me a jolt of anxiety.

I look cool on the outside, but on the inside, I've struggled to find my feet my whole life. The government came to our neighbourhood and wrote report after report, documenting the same findings over and over again but never doing anything with them. They wished us well but forgot that heaven and hell are not a destination for the afterlife . . . we were living in hell and the church folk that dropped onto our block to do prayer walks and then drive back to their gated communities in the suburbs were living in heaven.

"You make your bed, you gon' lay in it," my mom said on repeat. She basically trademarked it. With all the stuff we saw growing up and things we were a part of, she made it clear we would have to deal with karma—whatever energy we put out, good or bad, would always return to us. We would always get karmic payback, it was just a matter of time. But when it came, it came with some force.

Though we didn't have much, mom taught us how to save money and give back to the community. When money and work were good, she would save, buy groceries, and pay the bills. And she would donate to the food bank, because it was always there for us when she was between jobs. She was the definition of lifting others while you climb.

My mom was the most selfless person I knew. Mom was a goddess and a queen to every person in our household and everyone who knew her on the block. She was quiet but had a loud and soothing presence. She was Mother Nature.

She loved to crunch numbers and do quick math calculations when we ran errands together when I was growing up. Whenever she could, she helped me understand math in the real world. It was a competition every time to see if we or the cashier would get to the right answer first.

My mother was tender and cared for us kids, but she also cared for the other families on the block. She taught us always to show love to our people by checking in on them and taking care of those around us. In her eyes, being a prayer warrior was her third full-time job. At night, she prayed for everyone to make it home. She kept me afloat the times I stopped praying and always kept the house stocked up with Vicks VapoRub, herbal tea, cough syrup, and Ginger ale for when we got sick. And she always made sure we were stocked up with food and supplies in case there was a power outage or pandemic.

When we faced barriers, she taught us that we could always find a way, we just had to keep trying. With the odds stacked against us on the block, it was easy for the outsiders to label us criminals, but they didn't know what was really going on. To my mom, we were all still human. She remembered what everyone was like before the elements changed them. She never looked at anyone differently. I chose to have faith in her words when she said *they* were wrong about us. To her, our skin was not a barrier, it was our gift.

My mom was a genius just like all the Black girls I went to school with. They were geniuses and trendsetters in every and any category, but school staff often just thought they were loud, aggressive, or had too much attitude, which was far from the truth. The mandem were targeted in other ways, but it never came close to how my young sisters on the blocks were treated. We'd face microaggressions before we even had a chance to hang our backpacks in our cubbies.

Growing up in the hood we really had to fight for our education.

Often, the only time I would see my mom was when we sat on the couch watching TV together between her shifts. After a long day of work, I could see it in her eyes. She would always smile when she caught me staring at her, but I knew what that meant. Some weeks, she had no sleep in between morning and night shifts. But she suffered in silence. People say Black people—and more specifically Black women—are strong, but I never liked that because I didn't think it was the right word to use. While it seems like a compliment on the surface, it's really not. For many Black women around me, "strength" has an automatic association with silent suffering. I didn't want to hear that "you are so strong" narrative. Suffering in silence and emotional denial is not something to be celebrated.

My brothers and I put mom in a tough position when we got caught doing street stuff we shouldn't have been doing. Like many people around us, when we were kids we didn't learn the right way to honour, treat, respect, take care of, and protect all Black women at all costs. She, like many Black women around me, had a history of being everyone's everything at the expense of herself. I had to change this by supporting her anyway I could. At the time, we didn't know if it was depression, anxiety, or PTSD, but we knew that it was near impossible for anyone to be mentally untouched living in these environments.

I didn't see her much between shifts, but when I did, she squeezed in time for some ginger tea and some TV, mostly Black sitcoms—*The Fresh Prince of Bel-Air, Family Matters, Moesha, A Different World, The Cosby Show, Girlfriends, Martin, Sister Sister, The Bernie Mac Show, The Jamie Foxx Show, The Wayans Bros, The Parkers, The Famous Jett Jackson, Smart Guy*—or whatever was on TV. She always gave us a little bit of time and a whole lotta love. Enough to carry us for a few days until we chilled together again.

In my neighbourhood, we saw too much. Grandparents lived longer than some of their grandchildren. Bullets flew inches from our heads while we slept. Cops got angry and pushed people off balconies and out of moving vehicles. The SWAT team blew doors off their hinges. Some parents shot up after they got laid off of work and had no money for the bills. Children witnessed people foaming at the mouth in broad daylight in stairwells. Some parents pawned their own families items to get money to soothe their addiction. Families got eviction notices in the middle of the night. Children went to school hungry. Bullets took our friends right in front of our eyes. We watched our friends fight for each breath as if it was their last.

Our postal code and skin colour were an indicator of how we were treated in society. The broken concrete of our neighbourhood was stained red and filled with body bags and toe tags. And dreams that once gave us a spark were now faded. We were just kids. But we saw it all.

We had a hard time picturing a better life for our community, family, and ourselves because all we knew were the trenches around us. The feelings of hopelessness would cause us to reach for heaven because we felt like we were living in hell. Sometimes our heaven was drugs or another outlet to escape. PTSD, suicide, depression, and anxiety were real things I witnessed people struggling with but never talking about openly. I knew if we were honest about the things that were ripping us to pieces we would be able to save the lives of those around us or even save our own. Our external was a reflection of our internal and we were changed by the elements.

What if we talked more openly about mental health, PTSD, suicide, and depression? Would it change our relationships with ourselves and those around us? What if we talked freely about our feelings and emotions? Would it make a difference? Where do we get help? How can we help ourselves? Is it possible to heal in the same place we got sick?

These questions flooded my mind in 2004, after my cousin left a notebook of her depression and suicidal thoughts. She never had the chance to get help while she was alive. She felt isolated and alone, as if she had no one to talk to, judgement-free. She was only 20 and her life was just getting started. I was just sick and tired of putting my people to rest.

And while those around me were still alive, we were dying on the inside.

> *Death is not the greatest loss in life. The greatest loss is what dies inside while still alive. Never surrender.*
> —Tupac Shakur

When I was a child, I had many dreams of dying young. When I was in school, we had the "write your own eulogy" assignment. I took it seriously and wrote one of the best eulogies in my class . . . probably because death was something I thought about more than life. I knew nothing was promised, not even tomorrow.

Sometimes it was hard to know if I was awake or asleep because day to day what I saw with my eyes open were the same things I saw when my eyes were closed. Some days I wondered why I even tried to go to sleep. When I was a baby, sleep meant peace. But living in the hood, sleep and peace were distant cousins twice removed due to family drama.

These vivid dreams replaying reality made it feel like I hadn't slept in years; like I'd been awake too many days to count. PTSD and survivors guilt made my mind feel like a black hole that I had to struggle to crawl out of. Every time I had a source of light at my fingertips—something to hope for—I got sucked back into another black hole.

When we were young, we didn't talk about how we were hurting emotionally, but we felt it. Some days we wanted to leave and never come back to the block. And, at times, the thought of death would cross our minds as we woke and wished we were no longer living the life we were given. Some people were never the same after seeing the violence they grew up around, especially the kids.

Survivors guilt is what we're left with when we survive traumatic events that others around us do not. It's a mental condition. We had survivor's guilt.

When I was older, I would look back on my life and realize I never really knew my brothers or my parents as much as one should. When everyone was busy trying to secure the bag to pay bills and keep on the lights, it was left to the streets to raise me. We were family but circumstances didn't allow us to spend much time together. I would have to get to know them as an adult.

My mom woke up religiously, every day, for a double shift and saved up long enough to buy me a personal laptop at a time when they were limited in public schools and on the block. I was sleeping on the fold out couch from Grades 9 to 12 but my personal laptop gave me the upper hand, allowing me to work on projects for longer than the 20 minute time slots they gave us at the public library. My technology and my mom were my cheat code. They gave me access to an entire world of possibility in a neighbourhood where almost no one owned a laptop. Seeing my mom struggle made me want to have a better life for myself that would make her proud and give her an early retirement. I wanted to contribute around the house more, so I had to stay alive and try to make something of myself.

I was still running around with my homies, but I was slowing it down and laying low. We once did everything together—fought other blocks, hustled together, and took care of each other, but times were changing. Regardless of all that went down, as I got older, I felt safe at home on my block because I knew it like the back of my hand. I loved my hood and the people in it. I just had to be aware of the elements, know who was who, so I could be at least one step ahead of the game.

CITY OF TORONTO BUDGET AND FUNDING

YEAR	EMPLOYMENT	SCHOOL OPERATIONS	POLICE
2013	$69.0 million	$630 million	$1.02 billion
2014	64.0 "	650 "	1.08 "
2015	71.3 "	660 "	1.10 "
2016	70.5 "	660 "	1.13 "
2017	71.0 "	670 "	1.12 "
2018	65.8 "	680 "	1.13 "
2019	65.6 "	740 "	1.19 "
2020	63.5 "	770 "	1.22 "

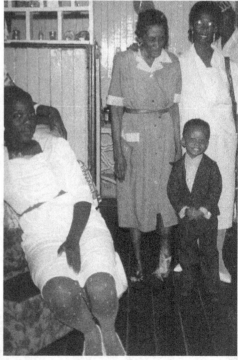

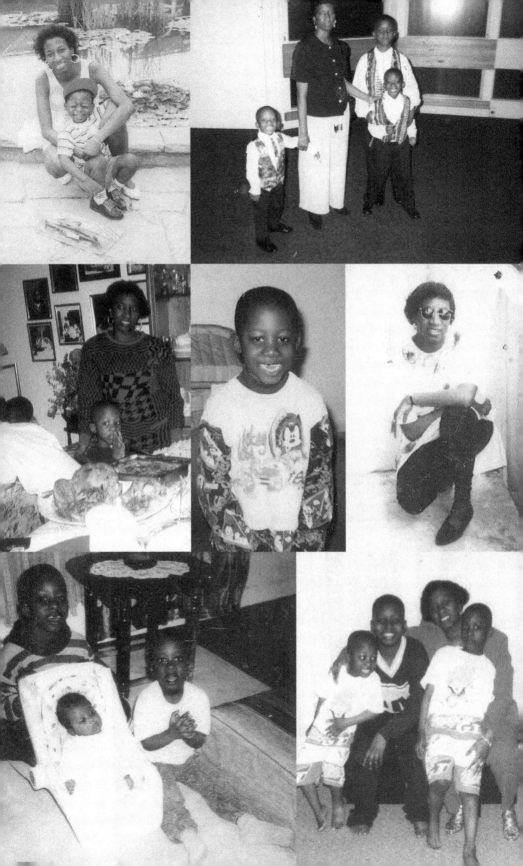

Them

This is for them boys and girls who get jailed
by schools and schooled by jails
Growing up a block away from Hell
A short stone's throw

This is for them boys and girls who step
foot in the church only for funerals
No bible study on Wednesday's
Gotta get them packs off, rent paid

This is for them boys and girls who march to grocery stores
in food deserts, leaving footprints of pain
Bonnets bop through the trenches

This is for them boys who can't sleep
till Mamma's company leaves
Couch = bed
Your back touching your cousin's knees

This is for them girls who get cat-called
She reports, then gets Blackballed
Due to her Black Scars

This is for them boys and girls
Drag you when your brows ain't done
Society demonizes your make-up
Still Beautiful

Unless we're shootin' no one notices the youth

—*Kondwani Fidel, Hummingbirds in the Trenches*

Hood Philosophers

Capital punishment means "them without the capital get the punishment."

—Bryan Stevenson

The majority of people who live in the hood aren't in the streets hustling like that. There is a small percentage of people who are actually out there, but we all get seen as one and the same.

Age 14: I saw young girls whose dreams were shattered when they weren't fast enough to outrun the stray bullets. My homie graduated college but attended graduation in a wheelchair after the chrome robbed him of his ability to walk for the rest of his life. I lost too many family members in hallways of apartment buildings and parking lots so I peep the rearview and side mirrors to stay aware of my surroundings. I came across the truth: receiving As in schools cannot stop strays.

Through the heavy L's we took we were still here. Still alive. Still breathing. Still fighting. That had to mean something. We felt the weight of every death across the city streets. To many of us, the city was a graveyard. But we had to keep going for those that we lost.

Despite what we experienced, some people in my neighbourhood saw what we didn't see: the future. In their eyes, if we didn't own our story someone else would; someone else would write the ending. To me, these people were hood philosophers. They were any and everyone in the hood who had wisdom about life, be they grandmothers, grandfathers, families that owned their own businesses, drug dealers, rappers, hustlers, or self-educated entrepreneurs. Hood philosophers were also people who were previously incarcerated or still in prison. What all these people had in common was the love they had for self-education, reading books, and putting what they learned into action.

Hood philosophers in my life were the people who experienced real hell in the trenches. Dre, who once taught me the ropes, dropped out of high school, but in prison he started to read books and expanded his vocabulary with words I had never heard before. Words like financial literacy, generational wealth, Black liberation, mortgages and real estate, marketing, mental health and wellness, group economics, anthropology, psychology, sociology, and Afrocentric history. He was now fluent in what money was and how to manage it, he understood credit and credit cards, and he knew how to register himself as a small business or corporation. And he gave this new game he'd acquired to the youngins . . . for free. He shared this wisdom even from behind the barred cages, preaching to us whenever he had enough money to call the mandem.

From the inside of prison, he gifted me a physical copy of a dictionary. It was a good starting point to learn new words and to open up some books to read as well. In his words, I needed to build up my reading muscles, then, when I was ready, he would suggest more books. I didn't fully understand everything he was saying but I believed him because he was saying things I had never heard before. Things that were never said in my neighbourhood. Though I didn't see him physically, the phone calls were enough to prove to me that he was different now than when he first went in.

Dre told me that the more words we know, the higher the level we could think on. And the higher the level we could think on, the less people could take advantage of us for what we didn't understand. He taught me "each one, teach one" which is an African proverb—when an enslaved person learned or was taught to read, it became their duty to teach someone else. I noticed similarities between his words and our experience; how we weren't given a financial education in public school. From my experience school did not reveal the truth but instead concealed it.

There was something in Dre's voice that I had never heard before. He sounded like he was in his own library in his own home. While I didn't understand all the words he was saying, I understood enough that it inspired me to not only start reading but try to better understand my life, community, and family. I wanted to find the words and books that interested me rather than the boring books assigned to us in school. I wanted something relevant, relatable, and something I would enjoy reading. I assumed if I read books I liked long enough, I could improve my reading level, which in turn would help me speed through the boring books that I was forced to read in school.

I thought I hated reading books because it felt like a death sentence, but in reality, I hated boring books. Now I was given a chance to read about topics I was more interested in.

Sometimes I couldn't connect to the academic writing because it wasn't rooted in the streets and didn't use simple language. That's why I liked Malcolm X, Assata Shakur, D. Watkins, Angela Davis, and Sister Souljah. Their words and writing showed me that they were out there on the front lines in activism but also in the trenches and the streets with and for the people.

I had no other option beyond what was happening around me, so I would keep that dictionary Dre gave me. I wanted to become more than a runner; I wanted to start selling on the curb and work my way up to having people work under me, like the bike shop. But Dre gave me and my other friends in the crew a hard no. Before he went to prison, he looked me straight in the eye and told me the streets weren't for me. He told me I would die out there. The OGs were in deep, but they gave me whatever I needed so I didn't have to hustle for money throughout high school. Whether it was food, clothes, sports equipment, school field trips, or extracurricular programs, they paid for it when my parents couldn't. It wasn't what I wanted to hear at that time, but I trusted Dre's judgment just as I did when he showed me the ropes of the corner.

Growing up, I saw the people who got sponsored by the corner. Now I was one of them. When they ate, we ate. This is how some of us were kept off the streets and encouraged to better ourselves in a school or wherever we put our energy. Though the hustlers felt stuck, they made sure not to give up on keeping some of the young ones away from the corner life. Where we lived, not many people cared about us, so we didn't treat the ones who did show love like dirt. They were all we had.

In my hood, showing emotion or a level of intelligence was seen as a form of weakness unless it was street knowledge that was being dispensed. But Dre was changing the game. He motivated me to leave the hustling and put my energy into something positive that could give me a good return on investment down the road.

I couldn't change my circumstances, but I wanted to take control of where I spent my time. I wanted to be different. I wanted a creative way to manoeuvre the block and level up in my life. It wouldn't happen overnight, but if I lived long enough, I knew I at least had a chance to see if it was possible. I was tired of trying to be someone else. I needed to find myself.

> *Would you rather be at peace with the world and at war with yourself, or at peace with yourself and at war with the world?*
> —Nipsey Hussle

> *Instead of trying to build a brick wall, lay a brick every day. Eventually you'll look up and you'll have a brick wall.*
> —Nipsey Hussle

Brokenness

I know too many broken
   people
broke into pieces
they think
they cannot fix.
Like shattered glass
they may cut you
when you try to uplift
slice the helping hands
hoping to heal
the harm
that has happened to them

They often hurt in silence
smile in your face today
and tomorrow
You may hear of how their
   brokenness
has escalated into acts of
   violence
Sometimes we judge the
   broken people
and call them names
label them, sometimes forget
that like flipping a coin,
they too can change.
But what does it really mean to
   be broken
When is it broken people
that have helped mend the
   world?

Realize that in our brokenness
is when our true lives unfurl,
My brokenness
gave me hope again
Transformed the shape of the
   world I knew
gave me a new beginning
allowed me to
recreate the world I live in

Brokenness is a sign of recreation
a sign of growth
but we fear brokenness
because we fear the unknown
and uncertainty
Brokenness
can piece our holes perfectly
Sometimes permanently

Afterall,
If you've never known
   brokenness
how will you know
when you are whole?
If you've never been broken
how would you measure
your growth?

—*Randell Adjei, I Am Not My*
   Struggles Poems

Hoop
Dreams

You may not control all the events that happen to you, but you can decide not to be reduced by them.

—Maya Angelou

July 2016: *One year before Ride For Promise*

O ur elementary school was filled with a majority of Black and brown kids from the block, but high school was a culture shock. We were no longer the majority. Birchmount Park Collegiate had kids from all across the Greater Toronto Area, some were from Toronto's housing projects, but there were a large number of rich kids from the Beaches and a high percentage of white kids. I could tell who was from the hood—not based on the actions of the students but rather on how we were treated and supported in school. If the students from the Beaches got caught selling a few dime bags, they received a warning. If the homies from my hood got caught doing the same thing, they got expelled immediately. With Black and brown kids, they had a zero tolerance policy and gave us no chances. There were no warnings, no calling your parents. This stuff I couldn't make up. These injustices were happening in the office, in the classroom, and in the hallways patrolled by hall monitors and cops. By the end of high school, almost all of the homies from my block were suspended, expelled, or transferred. The way the school was moving, it felt like it was a crime just to exist. We could literally catch a charge just trying to breathe the air. Regardless, we held it down in Cafrica, which was the name we inherited for the corners of hallways and the space beside the cafeteria where all the people from the blocks chilled. There were a couple of white dudes here and there but we still kept the name. Cafrica and the RISE room were the only places in the school the girls and the mandem could be themselves and just chill. At least until the cops came to ruin the party.

I treated high school as a fresh start, since many people there didn't know my story. I didn't want to get kicked out, so I pumped weights in the gym and studied in the library. I did anything I could to stop them from pinning something on me that I didn't do. My boys thought I switched up on them, but in reality, I was playing the long game and had to make sacrifices to try some new things. I knew they wouldn't all understand until we were older.

My homies were dropping like flies both in schools and in the streets.

On paper I did everything right—stayed in school, went to class, no longer sold drugs, graduated university, did extracurriculars, volunteered—but nine years later, at 23, I felt emptier than I did at 14 sleeping on the couch.

After high school, I went on to university and graduated from Queen's University and Ontario Tech University—receiving a physical and health education degree and an elementary teaching degree—but now I was back home, on the block, sleeping on the couch. The tragedy of my life was dealing with the shit that comes with being born into poverty, growing up in poverty, and still living in poverty after doing everything I was told to do. I came back with an expensive piece of paper and student debt the size of a down payment on a new Toronto home—even after playing Queen's University football as a starting slot receiver on an academic and athletic scholarship. I was popular on campus, but my pockets weren't fat like the majority of students there.

I was back to square one, living face to face with the street violence that was stealing the lives of those close to me. When we heard someone unload the clip, we knew it was time to run like we were about to miss the streetlights, because around here spilled blood doesn't dry. We felt those losses for life. They were engraved in us.

My five-year vacation in my own room at university was a dream. Once I got back to the block, university educated, I was back to sharing beds and couches with relatives until I could find a job and move out. To get some extra money, my side hustle was being a keynote speaker at events for youth and teachers, but I wanted to do something more with my life. I survived so much that I couldn't just call it quits. Especially now that I was back and my mom was still working.

She hadn't missed a beat. She was the key reason we always had food on the table and every bill was paid on time, no missed payments ever. I watched her stare blankly out the balcony window and I knew what she was thinking. Still here. Nothing has changed. The neighbourhood was still the same. The only difference was that we were all older. Now the little kids that I had been a camp counsellor for were in high school, and I was almost an OG. Many of my homies living on my block caught a case, were in jail, had kids of their own, or were dead. All before 25. Regardless, they were still good people. It was the elements in the streets that changed us. It was my mission to remember who we were before everything happened around and to us. Anytime we saw each other, it was all love. I knew the real them, not who they had to become to survive.

Free Game

The pursuit of knowing was freedom to me, the right to declare your own curiosities and follow them through all manner of books. I was made for the library, not the classroom. The classroom was a jail of other people's interests. The library was open, unending, free. Slowly, I was discovering myself.

—Ta-Nehisi Coates

The day after I got back to the block I received a phone call from the OGs. Dre was still in, but a couple homies who used to roll with him were freshly released from prison. They seemed different now, more educated than when they first got locked up. I knew I wasn't going back to hustling so I was okay with giving them some time to link on the phone. Blood or non-blood, we were all still family.

I don't remember much of what was said on the call, but all we talked about were books. And later that week, they dropped books for me to read into my mailbox. I felt like it was my first day of school all over again—street school. I was given books, news articles, and introduced to authors who were not available in our schools. I had resources on amazing Black women including Angela Davis, Audre Lorde, Assata Shakur, Maya Angelou, Sister Souljah, bell hooks, Robyn Maynard, Dionne Brand, Angie Thomas, Nic Stone, and Toni Morrison, to name a few. I had resources by Black men like Malcolm X, D. Watkins, Ta-Nehisi Coates, MK Asante, James Baldwin, David Chariandy, Kwame Alexander, Christopher Emdin, Marcus Garvey, Jason Reynolds, Ahmir Questlove Thompson, Fred Hampton, Kondwani Fidel, W. E. B. Du Bois, Wes Moore, Martin Luther King, Jr., and Walter Rodney. These were books that made me proud to be Black and gave me tools I couldn't get in school. They allowed me to see that change was possible.

Some of the books in my collection focused on grassroots activism, the importance of revolutionary thought, systemic racism, entrepreneurship, business, financial education, economic empowerment, sociology, and Black liberation. What stood out the most to me was the reality of the school to prison pipeline and that public school never taught us how to manage money, save money, invest money, understand credit and credit cards, and build enough wealth long-term that we could pass it on to the next generation. Money was the number one stressor in my neighbourhood and it was straight criminal to leave financial education out of our schooling. One unit or lesson on financial education was not enough. Self-education—finding the books and resources to educate ourselves—was the only option available to us.

When the former curb servers started recommending books, I remember quickly interrupting them and telling them I was trying to make money, I wasn't going to spend all my time reading books. They were dying of laughter, but they cleared their throats and went from joking to serious real quick. After they gathered themselves, they told me if I got smarter, I would get richer. They said "rich" didn't just refer to money but to all areas of my life—emotional, mental, physical, spiritual, and financial. This was brand new to me.

I had a light bulb moment after reflecting on our conversation and the book titles. All those book recommendations were not from the OGs who once rolled with Dre. They were from Dre himself. Despite being behind bars, he'd educated them just as he had me. He was giving us free gems for life and more education from inside prison than the teachers standing right in front of us in their overcrowded classrooms. Dre's love was real love.

In the world's eyes, he was a criminal, but in our eyes, he was a teacher.

The Power of Words

The schools we go to are reflections of the society that created them. Nobody is going to give you the education you need to overthrow them. Nobody is going to teach you your true history, teach you your true heroes, if they know that that knowledge will help set you free.
—Assata Shakur

I started to see and understand why, during slavery, if you were caught reading or teaching others how to read you would be beaten, killed, imprisoned, or even have your toes, fingers, or tongue cut off. One way people in power maintain control in society is keeping the people they control illiterate. They know literacy is connected to the liberation of the people, which is why it was illegal and a crime for slaves to read. As history has demonstrated, when people come to understand the level of social injustices they are faced with, they easily out-organize and out-strategize those in power and craft their own path to freedom. In many cases, they set themselves free in all areas of their life, not just physically. It became clear to me that the more words we know, the more we are able to organize our ideas. I started to see why these authors and thinkers were excluded from school libraries.

I learned from the streets, from the most unconventional teachers. While the school saw us as criminals, I saw us as people. People who made mistakes but were trying to get on the right path. And books seemed to make the difference, so I gave it a try. I didn't make it this far without mentorship, no one can truly make it alone. Without this village, I don't know where I would be. I was mentored by community leaders, my boy Julius, who was there for me in middle school, OGs, grandmothers, grandfathers, neighbours, dealers, inmates, parents, and those who did jail time. My mentorship really was the entire block. Nothing I did was an individual endeavour. Everything I had accomplished to date was communal. I couldn't forget my roots.

When I started to read I became sure of two things: 1) I am not responsible for the programming I received throughout my childhood and for the things that happened to me and around me, and 2) as an adult, I am responsible for finding new ways to improve my life and grow from what has happened. Although I couldn't unsee all the stuff that I had seen over my lifetime, I knew I was not alone. I was a product of my ancestors and my ancestors were the product of the books they read. They were self-educated.

Hanging up the Football Cleats

> *That speaks to me as a philosophy of living, that hope is a discipline and that we have to practice it every single day.*
>
> —Mariame Kaba

Reading was cool but putting things into action was better. Books gave me the power to reach for a future that I couldn't see but I knew was there.

Following the CFL draft, I was still speaking with a few teams about joining the practice roster. I knew I would have to work my way through somehow as I wasn't the best of the best in my graduating class, but I was a stone cold grinder. As a kid, I had thought playing professionally was the dream to achieve, but things started to change once I got back to the block as an adult after completing the Toronto Regional Canadian Football League Evaluation Combine. Though I was amongst the top performers for my position, I discovered that football was no longer my passion. It was my vehicle to escape the past I was running from. I only played because I was good at it.

I didn't know if hanging up my cleats was the right thing to do, but I did it anyways. At the time, I knew that the most important thing to me was my community and helping the young kids on the block who were doing drops like I had. I knew the best service wasn't lip service but direct service, so I made myself accessible to the block if they needed me while I figured out the next steps for my life.

I received an update from the community program on our block, Urban Promise Toronto, about the funding they lost for their after-school and summer programs. I came on board to lend a hand; I couldn't let down the little ones who were too young to understand this neighbourhood but looked up to me. Urban Promise didn't have much, but they gave kids a place to go. They had kept me off the streets in high school, gave me a job as a children's camp counsellor, and gave me supportive mentors and leadership opportunities, which kept me from feeling the pressure to hustle on the corner.

I had to do something outside of the box to challenge systemic racism and advocate for the rights of people who looked like me if I was going to make enough noise to get people to donate to the organization.

Dre called collect when he heard the news that I was planning to bike across Canada for the block. I had a year to plan and get fit. I couldn't just tweet about it; I had to do the work in real life with the community I was speaking about. In Dre's words, I had to keep moving my feet rather than my lips. Lots of people were retweeting and liking posts for activism, but outside of twitter, some of them did nothing. I had to be different.

Your mind is a weapon; you are never unarmed.
—Malcolm X

to Help Young People

Each One,
Teach One

> *The responsibility of a writer is to excavate the experience of the people who produced him.*
>
> —James Baldwin

Throughout my life, my brothers and I only knew a fraction of our parents' life story and journey before immigrating to Canada. We were family but strangers at the same time. We were adults before we finally had the capacity to take a breather from securing the bag and paying the bills to learn about the simple origin of our family.

"Can I ride your bike?" were the first words my mom uttered to my dad when they met as teenagers in 1978 in South America—Georgetown, Guyana, in a town called Kitty.

In 1989, in the early winter of December, my mom took a leap of faith and trekked to the far-off northern country and deep freezer known as Canada. With no knowledge of what winter or snow was, she arrived in her summer-ready island swag totally unprepared for the rude icebox that pruned her body upon arrival. A few years later my dad joined her, and they began to build their life together. Like many immigrant families, my parents didn't want us to just "get on our feet," they wanted us to hit the ground running and make a life for ourselves. Instead, we moved from public housing to public housing as my parents moved from temporary contract to temporary contract with the employment agency and factory jobs. Regardless of the instability, they always found a way to stay ahead of the bills, taking any opportunity they could get so they didn't need to look for help. The "glorious and free Canada" wasn't the life we knew. Even the immigrants that I knew with PhDs from their home countries were stuck driving us around in taxi cabs while my parents struggled to get on their feet. As new immigrants, the goal of achieving the Canadian version of the American Dream quickly became the goal of trying to keep our heads above water. The struggle was real.

One day, I found some photos of my mom salvaged from the basement archives. I discovered that she spent much of her childhood playing rounders—a game similar to baseball but with different batting rules—or spending time with the legendary Ma, her grandmother, who raised her. Her love for learning, reading, and spitting game to us that she got from Ma was her full-time job. All of Ma's mottoes and words to live by were drilled into the heads of my brothers and me. My favourite was "You don't miss the water until the well runs dry."

We started to hear stories about my dad, who was a professional cyclist as a teenager, competing with professional cyclists all across Guyana and South America. As an athlete transitioning from amateur to professional, he had a different reality than most of the cyclists, who had silver spoons in their mouths. He lived with his parents and nine plus siblings in a small town across the Demerara River outside of the capital, Georgetown. Cycling was expensive. The more money you had, the better the bike you could get. Compared to other cyclists, he had fewer gears and a heavier bike, but he trained enough to beat them consistently. He was all heart. Before I came into the world, he was known as one of the GOATs from his village when it came to racing, winning races against other pro cyclists as an up and coming amateur athlete, accumulating medal after medal—I started to understand why he cycled everywhere on his trusty bike any chance he could get.

With so many siblings, he did what he needed to do to help out around the house, even if it meant sacrificing his passions to provide for family. Leaving cycling behind, the remainder of his teenage and early adult years were spent transporting goods around Guyana as a way to bring in some money. That was my dad's non-negotiable responsibility—sacrifice your individual pursuits for the survival of the collective—but I knew he wished he could have found some way to keep riding.

My dad didn't have much to give us financially, but he gave us his most cherished possession—a love for cycling, bicycle engineering, mechanics, and business. The one thing in his life he had ownership over. It was clear why this brought him the deepest joy in his life. Sometimes I wonder what our relationship would have been if we had known this about him as children instead of as adults. As he was normally working three or more jobs, day and night shifts, we would only see him in the brief moments when he dropped off money, took us back-to-school shopping, helped us with our bikes, or taught us how to grow our own vegetables in the backyard. If we had understood that our 24/7 focus on securing the bag was a major reason we were all strangers in our own house, would we have been closer? I wondered if we could have had a bit more grace for him, his life, and what he and my mom had to juggle when arriving here in a foreign land without a blueprint or people to help along the way.

Thanks to my dad, the best memories I ever had were on a bike. My love of cycling was everything to me. I knew my brothers were also thinking the same thing. He taught us how to ride, fix, and maintain bikes as a way to pass on his love for cycling. Dad was determined to teach us how to ride our first bike and how to prepare the soil for growing our own fruits and vegetables, which were major parts of our lives. It felt like it was his life's purpose to teach us, because it was. We never quite understood that until we reflected on our childhood as adults.

I didn't realize it at the time, but ever since my ruby red BMX was kidnapped, every memorable moment in my life would happen with a bike. The summer I ran the first local bike shop business on my block over school break—with ten employees of my own; Dr. Alex creating his own motorcycle out of a lawn mower and a bicycle at 12 years old; the summer I got sponsored by local and national bike companies like Specialized Canada and Gears Bike Shop to compete in races across the provinces, aspiring to one day qualify for the age group Team Canada Duathlon team at the Multi-Sport World Championships. The summer I spent cycling coast to coast changed something within my father. It wasn't about me checking off a bucket list, it was my family's love of cycling that made this a family instead of an individual win. *When I pedalled, they pedalled.*

Growing up, one of the best fathers I knew was Uncle Phil from the *Fresh Prince of Bel-Air*. I would binge-watch it every day I could. Until now, at age 26, I had no deep connection with my dad. He was present and absent at the same time. I had mad beef with him because I didn't really know why he wasn't around much. I often heard stories from other family members, but I never heard an explanation from his lips. Today feels different. With a bird's-eye view, I can see my childhood and what happens when people juggle a million unstable factory jobs with limited financial knowledge and little education on how to make it here in this country. It all made sense, the struggling from paycheque to paycheque. He just didn't have the tools.

The bike meant everything to us. It was one of the only vehicles we owned as kids, allowing us to travel and see things beyond the few city blocks we called home. Reminiscing on every and any hustle we did on the corner, I can see that the bike not only helped me but saved my life. I learned valuable lessons from the streets in all areas of life: entrepreneurship, science, technology, engineering, arts, and mathematics . . . all starting with a single bike. With the bike lessening the great divide, we were no longer worlds apart from our dad. The bike was the foundation of our family. My first love. I didn't dig up all of his life as it still felt like we were strangers, but it was a start—a start at understanding the why and how between us.

Each one, teach one.

In our home country of Guyana, it's the norm to know your family members' full life stories—to know about your parents' upbringing and the impact of immigration on their lives. In Canada, on our block, we tend to know more about our friends than our families. I spent more time outside with my homies, co-parented by the streets.

The African blood pumping through the veins of my family and community naturally inclined us to move as one collective unit. This was the foundation and strength of our lives. But when we were scattered across Western countries, we lost our way and assimilated to the Western way of life that teaches every person for themselves. This way just doesn't work for the people in our hoods, especially for people who look like me. I knew I had to somehow change the narrative for the ones coming up. But first I had to somehow change myself.

My heart was heavy looking back at my life. Spending time with my brothers in my 20s, it seemed we were only now getting to know each other. All I could remember is that my brothers were my keepers from a distance. They taught me how to read the world and understand the streets when we left Regent Park and moved to Scarborough. They instilled the idea in me that we cannot wear our crown with our head down. I had to walk like I deserved to be on this earth. And for that, I was thankful. I was thankful to learn how to survive and make a name for myself amongst the chaos. We never spent much time together as they were busy trying to make money, but the advice was enough to keep me alive and aware of my surroundings.

My dad gave us his greatest gift in giving us the bike. Following in his footsteps, I knew I had to return the favour to the youngins coming up. I had no idea where to start, but the first step was continuing to be present and accessible to the block. The world was changing rapidly and becoming technologically advanced, and I knew that becoming a ghost to the block—never coming back to the hood to help the youth—was not an option.

I wanted to somehow become who I needed when I was younger.
Each one, teach one.

The Maritimes

Location: *Frederiction, New Brunswick (436 km from Halifax)*
4:30 p.m.: *Eastbound to Africville, Halifax, Nova Scotia*

I wanted to scream, but I felt like I was underwater. Tears started to ripple down my cheeks. The weight of the droplets felt so heavy, like I was crying blood. It had been 15 years since they last dripped down, but ironically, today crying felt good.

I was in the middle of New Brunswick, on the shoulder of the Trans-Canada Highway observing the transport trucks zooming by me, the smell of burnt rubber invading my nostrils as I battled to stay balanced on thin wheels that were quivering against the Maritime wind. My hands felt salty and sticky. My body was drenched head to toe like I just jumped into a pool. I had officially biked three-quarters of the way across Canada. I had been cycling 12 hours a day in the smouldering 35+ degrees Celsius heat—Caribana-type heat waves—which made me too tired to stop my mind from moving to the places and times in my life I'd rather not go.

Whenever I looked in the mirror I felt like I was staring at a stranger. I was the kid from the hood that many people said "made it," the rose in the concrete. University graduate, former CFL prospect, scholarship athlete, national award winner, valedictorian, community activist, the kid on TV bigging up the block, the list goes on and on. But all of it was fake to me. This was what people knew of me. They knew what I did but not who I was without all the accolades. They didn't know that after all those wins, after getting the degrees teachers told me to get, I was back on the same block, on the same corner where I first started hustling. What they didn't know was that I didn't truly know myself. After 24 years, I hadn't truly come to terms with who I am, the experiences I had coming up, what I saw, what I've been through and where I came from.

I tried to achieve myself out of trauma, but it wasn't possible. I was running. I was running from myself, but my past was in my shadow. As a child, I was not broken but I was changed.

I created this life. I tried to selectively block out memories of things I've seen, but as a consequence, entire periods of my life have been blocked out of my mind, including the positive moments I shared with families and friends on my block. Over the years, I became numb and couldn't quite remember anything about my childhood. But the experiences of my childhood, the person I was before all this "good" stuff happened, started to bubble to the surface.

My heart began to race. My pulse echoed throughout my body. The intensity increased. I no longer heard the cars and transport trucks flying beside me. The pressure on my head forced my eyelids to close, and my hands felt even more salty and sticky than they did before. My breathing escalated. From deep breaths to short breaths, I could no longer keep track of my heart rate. I had no control. For the first time in my life, I put aside my pride and the stigma of mental health. For the first time, I started to see that my mental health was a serious issue. Something I struggled with since I was in grade school.

With one-fourth of Canada left, I didn't know if I was going to make it, if I would continue riding. My mind was spinning. My head felt like it was about to explode. Travelling on a road bike all day, every day, all summer in this bent over position, my toes were squished and bleeding through the front of my Walmart socks. Muscle spasms were attacking my neck. My legs were dead. My back was without feeling. The skin on my hand looked like grated cheese, the handlebars ripping my fingers apart. I don't remember the last time I cut my nails or had a good sleep. I was out in the middle of nowhere, way too far from my hood in Scarborough, trying to bring some block motivation to inspire the youngins coming up. But what I really needed was to help myself. Some memories would be extremely difficult to swallow, but I knew they had to come back eventually.

This day, the person I thought I was died right in front of me. My sense of identity trampled. My neighbourhood experiences no longer forgotten. For most of my life, I felt like a directionless ghost, the sense of who I was and who I was trying to be felt like an illusion I could not grasp. I started to remember the systems and forces that destroyed and shredded my whole life, family, and community; the forces that made it difficult to get out of bed to go to school when I was a kid.

I started to remember the countless shell casings that skipped across the concrete on the blood-stained pavement. I remembered a community that took more losses of life than wins. We lived in a neighbourhood forced to survive with limited to no resources and opportunities in a nation mistakenly known across the globe for being "glorious and free." Anytime I heard glorious and free I always asked, "for whom?" The government had a historical legacy of underfunding our communities across the city and country and they needed to be held accountable for that. They had blood on their hands.

Were they "helping" us to break the cycle we were born into or were they doing all they could to ensure we are not able to break these chains?

The memories that started to surface made my heart race, but I was ready to face them. I was ready to remember.

I slowly started to recognize the roses, the beautiful parts of my community that had, for a moment, slipped my mind. But these roses were responsible for moulding me.

When I was losing my mind on the shoulder of the New Brunswick highway, I decided that I would continue to read and research global stories of hope every night. I was looking for people in similar communities who have discovered innovative ways to individually improve their own circumstances and elevate their community. I was searching for someone who out-strategized the systems and politicians who tried to erase our neighbourhoods. I needed to see an embodiment of what success looked like in the streets, stories that could help me see my life and my unhealed trauma differently.

In 2018, one particular story came up again and again. Not only did it change the way I saw my life, it changed the way I saw the world and human history. To this individual, people in the hood had to work with the cards they were dealt even if the people who designed their neighbourhoods took the whole deck for themselves. He was a person who changed his life first, then made sure he helped his entire community from kids, youths, adults, and families to those who were incarcerated or had run-ins with the law. He inspired the world with his own blueprint of what success really meant. To him, if we couldn't find an opportunity, we had to create our own. Taking life into his own hands, he found ways to get his hands onto books, education, and resources that weren't offered in the public education system. He essentially "read himself out of his circumstances."

In the words of the OGs, the real people to respect were queens who were queen makers and kings who were king makers, the real ones whose main mission was to help others level up and lift others as they climbed.

This legendary individual was known as Nipsey Hussle.

Hussle

People gotta express their struggle. When you ain't got no other means of liberatin' yourself, it's through spoken word and expression.

—Nipsey Hussle

Education must not simply teach work—it must teach life.

—W. E. B. Du Bois

E rmias Asghedom came into the world on August 15, 1985, in Crenshaw, Los Angeles, California. He was born of an African American mother, Angelique Smith, and an Eritrean father, Dawit Asghedom, who came to the United States seeking asylum. Growing up in the Crenshaw neighbourhood in South LA with his siblings, Samuel (Blacc Sam) and Samantha, his community experienced the ongoing impacts of police brutality, systemic racism, poverty, and racial segregation.

Governments underfund schools and community programs in low-income communities across the country and put more money into prisons than education. The school to prison pipeline is real. And the only people who benefit from this system are the corporations involved. In the United States, more people in the jail system means more money for the corporate players who own the prisons. In Nipsey's neighbourhood, kids from preschool to Grade 12 are being streamed into courses below their ability and routinely deal with the militarization of the police department, cuts to vital social and community programs, rising unemployment, and gun violence, all leading to mass incarceration and the many hardships that come with living in the streets of LA.

After listening to numerous radio interviews of Nipsey speaking on his childhood, I learned that he witnessed it all at a young age—robberies, people getting jumped at high school basketball and football games, riding his bike through the hood and getting shot at, young people being shot and killed right in front him, shootouts, people in and out of jail, and the reality of being treated like an inmate in schools with metal detectors and security guards that patrolled the hallways. With people losing their lives almost on the daily, it made sense why there was a strong internal pressure to be strapped for protection. School and prison were pretty much the same for many in his community, as it is in housing projects or low-income communities across the country. Though similar realities existed across the country, the communities in the streets of LA were unique as many communities were controlled by gangs that, at times, bordered different gang territories.

After being wrongfully accused of stealing computers from the high-school computer lab, Nipsey was sent to a juvenile program by the courts. Then, at a later date, he dropped out of Hamilton High School before graduating and, at 15, Nipsey joined the Rollin 60s Neighbourhood Crips gang based primarily in his home community. Before joining the 60s he was a straight hustler—riding his bike around the community to sell candy bars, bootleg software, music and movies, and hustling on the corner to buy anything he and his brother needed, such as fresh clothes, shoes, jewellery, and cars. In Nipsey's world, nothing was given to you. You had to grind for it.

Nipsey and his older brother grew up in their grandmother's house in South Central with his mother. He eventually became self-educated, reading books that weren't available in school and playing chess. With a mother who always kept books in the house and made education a top priority, he was well-versed and knowledgeable on many topics and subject areas. He first started reading things like magazines to learn about hip hop culture around the country, then found interest in other topics, like business. Nipsey made it his mission to read books and study the interviews of successful people so that he could be informed on subjects like Black liberation, Afrocentric history, sociology, psychology, anthropology, technology, holistic health, and nutrition. Through his self-education, Nipsey would discover a personal hero, Dr. Sebi, who was a renowned natural healer that used an African approach to health care. He also read books on STEM education, business, entrepreneurship, financial freedom, sales and marketing, financial literacy, investment, managing money, and building generational wealth so his family had money in the event that he was gone—all books and resources that are not available in public school in low-income communities across the United States, Canada, and Europe.

Most notably, he read books on the music industry and reached two conclusions: 1) as an independent artist you had more control over your career and got all the profits because you owned the rights to all of your music, and 2) as an artist who signed to a major record label company, you would sign away the rights to your music and profits in exchange for a big cheque up front. In the end, the record label owned your music and controlled the majority of your career until the contract was over. Under these 360 record deals, as they are commonly referred to, the only way artists can get money is through performing on tour or selling merch. This reading inspired Nipsey to make music full-time. He was now more educated on the business and the art of making music, putting himself in a place to make better financial decisions.

Living in LA, Nipsey was only able to see his mother's parents, so in 2004, when he was 19, his father took him and his brother on a trip to the East African nation of Eritrea for three months. Nipsey spoke in numerous interviews about how the trip changed his life and gave him more respect for women, community, family structure, and the dynamic between women and men. One of his key experiences in Eritrea was witnessing the value the community placed on collective rather than individual needs. Community members supported one another and cared for the well-being of the women. Living in America, with its culture of individualism and material gain, it was easy to accept the mentality of everyone for themselves, but in Eritrea, he experienced something different. This ended up being one of the turning points that led to his decision to become a community activist with a focus on entrepreneurship, technology, mental health and wellness, and financial literacy. Fast forward 15 years, and at 33, Nipsey had built ten plus businesses in his neighbourhood, primarily based at the plaza on Crenshaw Boulevard and West Slauson Avenue. This was the same street corner he grew up hustling and within the city he still called home. He would go on to build a family with actress Lauren London, their son Kross, and his daughter Emani.

Nipsey also talked in radio interviews about how some of his best ideas were inspired by the books he read. Self-education helped him stay in control of his music, money, and business, which meant no one could take advantage of him. He understood the importance of controlling and owning your own business—Black-owned business—and investing in the community so that other people have the opportunity to elevate their lives. I needed to break down his life, analyze his life moves, losses, challenges, and major life successes, for the people I was rolling with on my block, so we could understand his chess moves and draw inspiration from it for our lives. We broke it into a six-step blueprint that represented the key points of Nipsey Hussle's life and mission: Financial Literacy, Financial Empowerment, Entrepreneurship, Own and Control Your Story, Mental Health and Wellness, and Arts and STEM Education (Science, Technology, Engineering, and Mathematics).

This was how he, in his words, played chess instead of checkers. This was how he played the long game. He understood that each move in the present should get him closer to where he wanted to be in the long-term. To him, this was *the Marathon*.

The Blueprint

Financial Literacy (Music Career)

Most of the rappers I listened to growing up talked about buying jewellery, fancy cars, and expensive luxury brand clothing once they started making money. Nipsey Hussle, though, was built differently. The first time I encountered 21-year-old Nipsey Hussle was in an online interview on YouTube from 2006—one of the most popular videos at the beginning of his career. At the "Get Your Money Right" Hip-Hop summit in LA, he gave a public service announcement in which he said, "Instead of buying chains and cars, buy your mama a house and invest your money in real estate and assets. A real asset to take care of my peoples." With a quick Google search, I learned that investing in financial assets meant purchasing things that increase in value, putting money in your pocket instead of always emptying your pocket.

Like many people around me, money was one of the main stressors in our lives. Listening to Nipsey's story about coming up, it became clear that my community and I did not understand money the way he did. He saw money as a tool and he believed that once we understood how to use it and manage it, then we would be able to save and invest it to keep the money growing instead of going broke. If we understood that cash was our money and credit was someone else's money and we were just borrowing it, then we could figure out better ways to use credit instead of racking up thousands and thousands of dollars in credit card debt. Unless we understood how to manage money and the power of credit we would continue to struggle financially in the short- and long-term.

In 2008, during the years of the global financial crisis, Nipsey signed his first record deal with Cinematic Group and Epic Records. One week after signing, he spent 60 days in the county jail, but when he was released, he was motivated and started dropping album quality mixtapes. In 2010, he left Epic Records and became an independent artist, creating his own record label company called All Money In Records—a business with his family, Blacc Sam, and his founding partners and friends Stephen "Fatts" Donelson and Adam Andebrhan. This began his journey of Black ownership, unity, and self-sustainability as he followed the principles of the company, *all money in, no money out.* The company mission statement emphasized the importance of keeping every dollar circulating in your community, saving and investing your money to build generational wealth rather than spending money on materialistic things. This was how they economically revived low-income communities like his neighbourhood of Crenshaw through restorative investment and self-empowerment.

As he began his music career, he did everything himself—recording, engineering his own music, marketing, sales, and distribution—but once his money grew, he built a team to help him become a music and business mogul. Nipsey Hussle's entire body of work includes 13 full mixtapes, 49 singles, three compilation mixtapes, and one Grammy-nominated studio album, *Victory Lap,* which was released in February 2018.

One thing that stood out about Nipsey's music career was his *Crenshaw* mixtape. When he began selling physical copies of the CD for $100 each, it went viral online as people rushed to see why he was charging so much per mixtape. Nipsey got the idea from the book *Contagious,* which talks about a Philadelphia restaurant that sold a $100 philly cheesesteak sandwich. The idea was so crazy that everyone started to talk about it and the buzz grew. People started coming from around the country to try the sandwich, bringing in a lot of business and a lot of money. Word of mouth is great marketing. Like the philly cheesesteak sandwich, Nipsey's mixtape was a success. After launching a documentary to promote his *Crenshaw* mixtape, he revealed a limited quantity of a thousand CDs for his first batch of sales. The CDs sold out in less than 24 hours—including a hundred copies sold to JAY-Z—making Nipsey $100,000 in less than a day. As an independent artist and record label owner, he had full control of his art and money, which means he didn't have to give anyone a cut of his profits.

One of his first studios was in his childhood friend's bedroom, which had motivational quotes written on the walls in permanent marker: *If you want it, go get it. Quitting is not an option. Don't talk about it, be about it. Kill them with success. Don't wait. There will never be the perfect time.* They would need this motivation years later when their upgraded studio, filled with equipment worth over $100,000, got raided and the police took everything. They built their next studio from scratch, which took a year from start to finish, but then they were evicted. Nipsey and his team were given two days' notice and were then escorted out by the police. They never missed a rent payment, but they didn't realize they were subletting rather than renting the property—they thought they were paying the landlord, but they were paying someone else. As a result of the paperwork confusion, they were kicked out and had to start from scratch again after losing everything for the second time. They faced many barriers but continued to follow the motto that became a major part of his globally recognized brand: *The Marathon Continues.*

Nipsey never talked just to talk. He followed his own advice and transitioned from hustling and gang culture to global entrepreneur, philanthropist, activist, and artist. He knew there was more to life than gang culture and conflict that was passed down from generation to generation. What I appreciated most about him is that he talked openly about his street life in his music from beginning to end. Listening to the progression of his music, from the first mixtape to the last album, it was clear that he let go of some habits and started to grow and try new things. His story inspired those around me to be smart with their money and to take care of themselves and their family long-term—generational wealth.

In his spare time, as a forward thinker, he educated people on cryptocurrency and the changing financial world and motivated others to educate themselves to stay equipped for the future. His philosophy was that life is a marathon not a sprint, a long-distance race focused on endurance and unshakable faith. Life is a long-distance race that honoured those who never quit and stayed ten toes down until the end.

His success was impressive, but what put his musical career into perspective for me was that he still had to manoeuvre the reality of his neighbourhood. Over the course of his 11 years of promos, recording music, and touring the world, he'd lose many friends and family members to gun violence and the school to prison pipeline.

Financial Empowerment and Entrepreneurship (Community Investment)

Hussle got his nickname from his spirit of entrepreneurship. At age 11, he began shining shoes for $2.50 per pair with a goal of shining a hundred shoes a day, seven days a week. His mom worked long hours to support the family and paid the bills, but he and his brother had to hustle to get money for things they needed, like additional food, gas money, name brand clothes, and rent once they became teenagers. It was this inspiration and motivation that led him to creating businesses as an adult and entrepreneur in this community.

Nipsey Hussle and his All Money In team started, owned, and operated the following businesses: The Marathon Agency (branding, marketing and media agency), The Marathon OG (a Nipsey Hussle collaboration to produce his own exclusive marijuana), The Marathon Cultivation (marijuana company), Baba Leo's Fish Shack restaurant, Steve's Barber Shop, Elite Human Hair (selling bundles of premium extensions and hair pieces), Wireless Connection (a cell phone shop), The AMB store (All Money Business clothing company founded by Hussle and best friend Cobby Supreme), and he had a business partnership with the popular fast food franchise Fatburger.

With his brother, Blacc Sam, Nipsey also opened The Marathon Clothing store (formerly called Slauson Tees), and later, inked a brand partnership with Puma and The Marathon Clothing. Nipsey got the clothing idea from his brother, who saw opportunities that other people didn't see. But he didn't stop there; he made the clothing store the "world's first smart store aka the Apple Store of the hood." When customers visit the storefront, they experience exclusive music and interactive visual content through an augmented reality mobile app—the TMC Smart Store App—created by Iddris Sandu, a software engineer from Compton. By scanning labels located throughout the store and on shirt tags, people would have an interactive experience played on their smartphone.

In addition to these businesses, Nipsey also had a number of partnerships and investments. He started a business partnership with David Gross—a successful investment banker in New York who grew up in South Central—for S.C. Capitol Ventures, specializing in urban development and investments. Their first investment was the renovation and reopening of World On Wheels, a skating rink in LA that had closed in 2013. He spoke, throughout his music, to the importance of life insurance and learning about cryptocurrency. Nipsey himself had a cryptocurrency business, was an investor in Vezt (the first mobile app that allowed music fans to share royalty rights for songs and recordings by artists they love), partnered with cryptocurrency company Follow Coin, and later bought a fish market in his community. He also, in collaboration with Puma, donated a brand new basketball court to the local school in Crenshaw.

Of his many business moves, there are two that are most notable. The first was becoming the co-founder of Vector 90, an inner city co-working space and business incubator focused on developing underrepresented entrepreneurs. It was designed specifically to give entrepreneurs from the community their own office space to work on their businesses, meet other people, and network. As people interacted with others, exchanging information and developing professional and social contacts, they were given an education in entrepreneurship, support launching their start-up organization, and opportunities to pitch their business for the chance to win funding for their company. The beauty of this space was that it was located right in the neighbourhood where Nipsey grew up, so community members didn't have to travel hours to get to other co-working spaces outside their neighbourhood.

The second notable business move was the $2.5 million purchase of the strip mall plaza with his business partners David Gross and Blacc Sam that housed a few of his businesses, including The Marathon

Clothing store. With this purchase, he became the owner of the same plaza he grew up hustling out of at the intersection of Crenshaw Boulevard and West Slauson Avenue. He no longer paid rent, instead, businesses in his plaza paid him rent. Without a doubt, I understand why the city renamed the corner of Crenshaw and Slauson *Ermias "Nipsey Hussle" Asghedom Square*. He was a certified street legend and global icon.

As an owner of all these businesses, Nipsey could make music at the studio, get a haircut, buy some food at the restaurant, purchase a new phone, get new swag, and have business meetings for free because he owned all these services. His life symbolizes the power of Black ownership and the importance of community redevelopment that's led by the community, for the community—for us, by us. He saved up his money and reinvested in himself and his community, elevating everyone around him.

In every and all interviews, the humility and graceful presence of Nipsey always shone through. He never missed the opportunity to shout-out to his brother, Blacc Sam, who he credits with being his biggest inspiration and the reason for his success in business since they were kids. In highlighting the behind-the-scenes support of the All Money In team, his family, his community, and his business partner David Gross, he showed the power of one team, one voice, and one vision.

> *You don't need to be a voice for the voiceless. Just pass the mic.*
> —Dr. Su'ad Abdul Khabeer

Nipsey took the mic and told us about his life and the plight of his community. As an independent artist, he controlled the narrative from start to finish. He was not a social media activist. He practised what he preached and was on the front lines with everyday people. He was a model for the world for how to control your message, stay authentic, and be yourself unapologetically. Along the way, he inspired people to see that there was more to their life beyond their present circumstances. Some rappers write music about a life they haven't lived, but Nipsey lived the life he talked about throughout his music. By speaking for himself and his neighbourhood, he set a standard and inspired others to live differently. He set an example to follow and displayed his growth, graduating from gang member to international artist, entrepreneur, community activist, revolutionary, philanthropist, business mogul, and owner of several real estate properties.

He created a culture of entrepreneurship in his community, which meant new opportunities and more options, giving people something to strive for other than street life. He didn't only teach people how to fish; he gave them fishing rods and the other tools needed to fish. He embodied the words of Maya Angelou: "When you learn, teach. When you get, give." For Nipsey, it was about mobilizing his people to unlearn their way of life and relearn a new way of living that could help them build a better life for individuals and their family. Nipsey became the person his younger self had needed and an example for the world to follow. He gave others opportunities so they didn't have to repeat the mistakes of previous generations in gang culture. Nipsey remained accessible to the community no matter how far he went, which brought real change to his neighbourhood and city—and echoed worldwide.

His body was taken, but no one could ever mute his spirit.

STEM Education (Science, Technology, Engineering, and Mathematics)

I for one believe that if you give people a thorough understanding of what confronts them and the basic causes that produce it, they'll create their own program, and when the people create a program, you get action.

Malcolm X

Nipsey was a forward thinker and knew that STEM education was the future. Tech advancements are happening so fast worldwide that there are more jobs available in the STEM industry than there are people qualified to fill these jobs. He knew the jobs that exist today for many working-class people in his community and worldwide would soon disappear and be replaced with technology—cashiers replaced by self-checkouts, music and video stores replaced by streaming services.

Nipsey identified that STEM education opportunities were non-existent in communities like his across the entire country. He knew that STEM education was a way to financially empower the neighbourhood, and without this education, the community would get left behind. This is where Nipsey and his team came in.

The gaps that already existed between wealthy white communities and low-income Black and brown communities were massive, and Nipsey knew this would drastically increase as a result of this lack of STEM education. So Nipsey and his business partner, David Gross, decided to create Too Big To Fail. This STEM education academy for inner city youth would be operated in combination with his business Vector 90. This centre would bridge the gap between inner cities across the US and Silicon Valley, a global centre for tech and one of the wealthiest areas in the world. Nipsey's work would increase diversity in STEM and give low-income communities, girls, and Black and brown youth the opportunity to have a community-based program tailor-made for them.

His life was bigger than music. In partnership with David Gross, who also grew up in LA, Too Big To Fail and Vector 90 was one of the first community-based co-working spaces and incubators with a STEM education centre in the world. And it was operated by people he hired from his neighbourhood. Music was his passion, but his life's work was always bigger than just rap. Investing in his own community, creating opportunities, and providing resources to empower the hood was a major part of his mission.

Nipsey knew talent was universal but opportunity was not. And since tech was one of the most profitable industries, he made sure to provide kids in his neighbourhood with new opportunities that could better prepare them for the future. He was just one person, but he gave his community all of the opportunities he didn't have access to growing up.

Mental Health and Wellness

People did whatever they had to do to survive and put food on the table, pay their bills, hustle for school clothes, and take care of their family. With this reality, it took people like Nipsey to empathize with the situation and provide his own solutions for the community. He recognized that living in the hood and dealing with this chronic stress had a negative impact on people's emotional and mental health, and that this affected the quality of life and relationships. So he came up with his own solution to lessen the psychological stressors, thereby helping others live a better life. One way was providing his community with multiple businesses that gave jobs to local community members who found it difficult to secure employment elsewhere, including local artists, the elderly, youth, those who had spent time in prison or had run-ins with the law, and even world famous neighbourhood legend Slauson Bruce. His community investments and rehabilitation of buildings in the neighbourhood were an act of healing for the people as he made new opportunities available that positively impacted the mental health and well-being of his block.

Nipsey put his life on full display in his lyrics, talking about the survival strategies he needed growing up and how he made a conscious choice to evolve from those habits so he wouldn't stay in the same pattern when he was older.

People who live in poverty and have limited to no resources are put into survival mode. Our focus is to survive by any means. When people are hungry, when they have to search for ways to get food, school supplies, clothes, or merely pay the bills to keep the lights on, mental health suffers. Nipsey hired people from the community and gave them educational opportunities that could prepare them for the future. These options benefited the overall health of the community and improved the mental health and well-being of the neighbourhood because the people he employed didn't have to put their lives, their freedom, or the security of their families on the line to get money. Nipsey created jobs and gave community members the opportunity to elevate themselves and their families financially in an area with limited employment opportunities.

Growing up in my hood, we never talked about mental health, mental illness, or the impacts of PTSD, depression, and anxiety. So often, we'd hear about these issues in rap music and hip hop culture from artists like Nipsey Hussle, Lauryn Hill, Meek Mill, Roddy Rich, Mereba, John River, Noname, Shad, Nas, Tupac, J. Cole, and others. They offer open and unedited stories about the challenges they've had with their mental health and the heartbreak of witnessing those around them struggling to survive or living paycheque to paycheque. These artists and others were able to express what was happening in a way that I couldn't. Through their lyrics, I started to learn about mental health and that it's okay not to be okay.

The way they talked about mental health was more encompassing than anything I heard in school. These lyrics didn't cure me of all the trauma and pain, but they did show me the first step I needed to take towards improving my mental health. This first step was acknowledging that the things I have experienced and seen in my past still impact my mental health today. Looking around my block and listening to rap music, I learned that I'm not alone and that many are in the same boat.

We were always capable of doing good, we just needed the tools to do better. And if we couldn't get those tools in school, as Nipsey told us, we had to find the tools for ourselves. We had to be wise enough to pick up information as we go. Whether it was the library, Internet, books, YouTube, podcasts, interviews, learning from our surroundings or other people's stories, we had to do anything and everything to get the information we needed to level up.

The power of stories gave Nipsey a different perspective on how to change his life for the better and improve the lives of people around him. He was living proof that self-education was one of the only ways to holistically improve our life and community.

Self-starter

Nipsey was the definition of a start-up organization. As a resourceful child, when his family computer broke down, he read computer magazines and books and built a working computer from scratch with the spare computer parts he gathered from the community so he could continue making music and beats. From a self-starter who sold T-shirts out of the garage, mixtapes out of his trunk, and hustled on the curb, he transitioned to owning his record label, a clothing company, real estate properties, a cryptocurrency business, and a community business and tech hub. The way he was moving, he was literally buying back the entire block, calling all the shots, and rehabilitating the neighbourhood instead of letting gentrification—led by people not from the community—destroy, evict, and displace the Black community after they invested in the neighbourhoods.

Nipsey was a human library, using the information he gathered from his self-education and putting it into action. The more books he read, the more he filled up his internal library. Throughout his career, he spoke to how books helped him navigate the systems that were designed to keep his neighbourhood and people boxed in. Society gave him a script to follow based on his zip code and skin colour, but he ripped that stuff up and made a script of his own.

Unity was once the fine fabric of our people, the people on my block, who represent a cross-section of the African diaspora. But when our families encountered Western culture and were forcibly moved or migrated to places like Canada and the US, this mentality changed, becoming more about "everyone for themselves." Throughout history, unity amongst marginalized and specifically Black communities has been a threat to those in power, and unity is what Nipsey was after. Those in power designed poverty as a straitjacket for us, so the odds aren't in our favour, but it was refreshing to see Nipsey take things into his own hands and do it with the people he was often told were the wrong crowd. Nipsey was different because he gave educational lessons for free. His rap lyrics and his interviews were filled with gems on financial education, entrepreneurship, technology, marketing, Afrocentric education, and the importance of learning about the work and life of Dr. Sebi. At the core of his work, shared freely, were the tools and skills that he had used to rebuild his entire community and help others help themselves.

When you don't know who you are, it's difficult to find a place that feels like home.

Nipsey focused on changing his world first before changing the world. He focused on his life and family and then his community. In the end, he had a powerful impact on the world and spread his views on what real community-based change looks like when it is funded, controlled, and operated by the people who live in the community. He didn't wait for people to give him a seat at the table. He built his own table. He built his own house. And he owned the whole neighbourhood block. With that power, he brought in his own people to sit at his table so they could build together for the people, the children, youth, elderly, the families and single parents, the formerly incarcerated, the mentally ill, local artists, entrepreneurs, small business owners, the people looking for homes and places to live, and more. This was the power of ownership—Black ownership—and the power of investing in your community.

Nipsey taught the world a different way of living instead of just applying for a job. He taught the way of entrepreneurship and investing in yourself and your community by finding new ways to make money, build businesses, and build a solid foundation for your family to eat long-term. He wasn't perfect, no human being is, but he showed us what it means to be truly human. He was pure. He was a compass. And he redefined success. Success wasn't all about making it out of the hood. Success was about making his life and his hood better. Whether people were gang members, inmates, or had pasts they weren't proud of, to Nipsey, they could still have an opportunity to change and make a positive contribution to this life. To him, it wasn't a crime to evolve.

Standing tall at 6 foot 3 with a body full of tattoos and a neck full of jewellery, including a gold chain of Malcolm X, his first name, like his life, was prophetic. Ermias translates to *God will rise*. Looking at his life, it's clear why he was invited to numerous universities and colleges to be a guest lecturer and professor. In many ways, when I think of Nipsey Hussle, I also think of Chadwick Boseman, who played the world's greatest superhero, Black Panther. Through the Marvel Studios movie, *Black Panther,* Chadwick showed the entire world, people across the African diaspora, and specifically Black people, that with or without the superhero suit, once we realize who we are and what we are capable of, we have the power to change our lives and our communities.

Growing up, we thought the only options were to get a job or hustle on the corner, but through people like Nipsey, our eyes have been opened. With access to information we didn't yet have, we could build our own businesses as a side hustle, part-time or full-time.

There is not one single answer to what goes on in hoods around the world because we do not live single-issue lives. But Nipsey showed us the importance of providing an ecosystem of resources and opportunities and jobs to local community members. He and his team rehabilitated an entire community and did more for these neighbourhoods than the government has ever done. This was hyper local change that made a difference, not just lip service. He was somebody who cared enough to invest in people to create real change.

As a member of the Rollin 60s, he was still in the neighbourhood, but he was serving the street corner in a new way. Nipsey Hussle is a global icon, and most importantly a street legend. A legend whose passing started to unite communities—regardless of colour and gang affiliation. Nipsey helped us see that the systems that designed our communities and left people to survive these streets were the real force to fight against, not each other. In his honour, David Gross, his business partner and close friend, is continuing their joint plan and

Nipsey's legacy by bringing the same change to hoods all across America. Their initiative is called Our Opportunity and Own Our Own—an economic stimulus program and investment fund, starting in California with plans to go nationwide, that raises capital to invest restoratively into Black communities, entrepreneurs, and businesses that have historically received little or no investment across the country. In addition, to finish off what Nipsey started, Blacc Sam and the Hussle team will continue to finish the Nipsey Hussle Tower which is a mixed-use residential building that will provide affordable housing upstairs and commercial space on the main level at the corner of Crenshaw and Slauson where they grew up.

Reminiscing on my life, I started to identify all the transferable skills and abilities we had on the block and on the curb. Once I dug deeper and saw the entrepreneurship skills knitted into the fabric of the community, I saw my neighbourhood and the people differently. I didn't just listen to the words of Nipsey Hussle through his music and interviews, I studied him. I dissected his blueprint for success as he spoke the language of the streets in words that my homies and I could understand. What was most impressive about Nipsey wasn't only his success, but the origin of his story—the come up of how he tapped into his inner creativity and entrepreneurship skills in the hood to make a name for himself and his people. He was more than a neighbourhood hero; he was a global icon and hero who passed power to his people and paved the way for those in the streets to make change and take control of the narrative of our lives and communities. Nipsey Hussle's life is a story that should be required reading in every facet of society as he is the textbook example of lifting others up as he climbed. No artist in history has holistically lifted up their own neighbourhood and channelled the power of hip hop and entrepreneurship back into the community like Nipsey Hussle. He was the Tupac of our generation.

Where we came from, the only way to believe in the future was to take the responsibility to create it for ourselves.

Africville

There is a tradition amongst people who cycle across Canada to dip their front bike tire into the Pacific Ocean on the shores of Vancouver to symbolize the start of their cross-Canada ride. They would then do the same, dipping their front tire into the Atlantic Ocean, when they reached the finish line in Halifax, Nova Scotia. But for Ride For Promise, it was going to be different.

Bligh and Trey were now our two drivers, replacing Cameron who had to go back to work. Bligh and Trey were responsible for driving us safely from Toronto to Halifax to finish the journey. They were my high school homies and I trusted them to help our team finish what we started.

I met Trey in Grade 8 when we played on the same basketball team and won the provincial championship in our division. He played both point guard and shooting guard, which was fitting for the type of person he is. He's calm, cool, and collected and is still one of the wisest people I've met. He's the type of person that would hit game winning shots and just smile, no excessive celebrations. Anytime Trey spoke, everyone would listen. He never wasted words and never did any long talking. WWTD, What Would Trey Do, was the thought that crossed my mind when I was doing something stupid during a basketball game—or in life. Through our friendship, he taught me the importance of protecting my energy at all costs and taking care of myself and those close to me. He comes from a Jamaican family and was raised in Scarborough where he still lived. He's a real one and was a special part of the team.

I met Bligh in Grade 9. We were both part of the Birchmount Exceptional Athlete program (BEAP). Athletes from all across the city would attend our school for this elite program, which was supposed to prepare us to excel in provincial and national sport. This program gave many of us the ability to get athletic scholarships in university and produced numerous pro athletes. Bligh is another wise soul and always straight business. He reads books faster than anyone I know. In high school, he was knowledgeable about mental health, financial education, and fitness, and he got good grades. He meditated, did yoga and mindfulness, and he saved his money, invested money, and had a great credit score—all while being an avid hip hop fan and someone who was proud to be Black and educated on his African roots. He always reminded me that our history started with kings and queens and not slavery, which I knew but wish I had understood better as a child. Born of a Trinidadian family, he was also raised in Scarborough and still lived there.

I wouldn't have finished Ride for Promise without Bligh and Trey. Without them by my side, I might have quit back in New Brunswick when I was losing my mind. Their perspective on life and mental health gave me the energy to finish what I started. It was their idea to end the trip in Africville, which made all the difference. This community's story is a testimony to the experiences of Black Canadians coast to coast.

We were the only documented ride in history doing it for the hood so we decided to finish not in Halifax, but in Africville, because despite being erased, physically and from the text books, the ancestors and descendants of the community were keeping the memory of Africville alive.

One of the first free Black communities outside of Africa were in Nova Scotia. Africville was one of these communities. Located on the northern shore of Halifax Harbour, on the Bedford Basin, it was a lively Black community for more than 150 years. Founded in the mid-eighteenth century by Black Nova Scotians from a variety of cultural origins, many of whom were formerly enslaved African Americans, the community was filled with brightly painted houses that snuggled into the hillside of Halifax, surrounding a small pond where kids went fishing and boating on rafts.

In the 1960s, in an act of politically motivated racism, the community of Africville was destroyed by the government to make way for "urban renewal," that is, the installation of the A. Murray MacKay Bridge, a suspension bridge that connects Dartmouth and Halifax. They forced residents of Africville and their descents to relocate, bulldozing many homes in the middle of the night while families were still inside. Many Africville residents owned their homes and land and paid city taxes but were still denied the services other white communities received, including proper running water, sewage disposal, paved roads, garbage removal, health services, street lights, electricity, police services, fire services, and a cemetery. While these services were being denied, the Canadian government was relocating the slaughterhouse, garbage dump, and hospital for infectious disease near Africville in an effort to harm the community. As a result of this violence and forced removal, the Africville community was scattered and many people were relocated to public housing.

This treatment was not new to Black people. Time and again, Canada has demonstrated that it values property more than people and has a dark history of destroying and seizing the land of Indigenous and Black communities coast to coast, a dark history that continues into the present day. A simple Google search will tell you that Canada and the United States are a lot more similar than mainstream media and school textbooks tell us. The last home in Africville was destroyed in 1970, but the government didn't acknowledge the wrongs they did until 2010, when they issued a public apology. Destroying people and communities then apologizing for it after the fact is the only Canada I know. Apologies are as Canadian as maple syrup. Now Africville has been replaced by Africville Park where the residents and their descendants gather each summer with their family and friends to remember and celebrate their community.

Today, the community is still fighting for justice and not to be forgotten. Some settlements were reached and an Africville museum was established, but this doesn't make up for the destruction of a thriving community whose only crime was being Black in a country that's been painted white. This is the Black experience in Canada. This is not just part of Black history, this is Canadian history. This is Canada today. Reparations are still needed.

What happened to Africville makes me think of the forced relocation and destruction of low-income communities across the city of Toronto. Communities are destroyed to make way for more and more condos or government initiatives that don't serve people who look like us. Neighbourhoods are forever changed. The places we live, play, pray, and even lost our loved ones are distant memories. With new high-rises blocking the skyline view and destroying the natural environment in hoods across the city, our communities are now unrecognizable. We are slowly being pushed out and erased, which is why fighting to keep the stories alive is more than just storytelling. It is preserving the past, present, and future.

The Finish Line

Location: *Tatamagouche, Nova Scotia (150 km from Africville)*

8:00 a.m.: *Eastbound to Africville, Halifax, Nova Scotia*

It felt like yesterday that I was in Vancouver. I had no clue what would happen along the way; I didn't even know if I would make it. Much of my approach to the trip was like a freestyle battle. I just woke up. No rehearsal. I just went straight from the dome. On social media, we looked polished. Our followers saw our posts about arriving in new cities and small towns, speaking at different venues, in churches and parking lots, but we dealt with challenges and hiccups that we weren't able to post. In reality, most days we knew the destination but had no clue how we would get there. On any given day, we had 12–15 hours to figure it out. Most of the time, I got lost, a bike tire popped, the cell phone had no signal and the team wasn't able to locate me, and our car broke down. At the end of the day, the issues we faced along the journey didn't matter anymore because we were almost at the finish line. All I had to do was finish what I started.

I was 150 km from Africville. One ride from finishing this ride across the country. I could still remember riding up the mountains and swimming in sky blue lakes that I had only seen in movies. I saw the mountains and evergreen forests that hug British Columbian cities and the rolling farm fields of the Prairies. I cycled around the interconnected freshwater lakes of the Great Lakes in Ontario—Lakes Superior, Huron, Ontario, and Erie. I survived long enough to make it to the province of Quebec and experience the cities known for poutine. From the beautiful sunsets on the west coast, to the ocean breeze on the east coast, headed to the finish line.

With the cars zooming by me and the tsunami of rain puddles soaking my entire bike, I had to squint to see through my foggy glasses. My body was drenched head to toe and my hands were freezing. I was cheesed. I was cycling to Africville from Tatamagouche, Nova Scotia. I had no clue where I was and I couldn't pronounce the names of the towns I was passing. All I cared about was that 150 km to Africville meant 150 km to freedom. I was no longer wide-eyed and smiling ear to ear as I had been in the beginning. I just wanted to finish, go home, and K.O. for a month at least. I wanted to retire from all exercise for the next five years.

As I squinted through my foggy sunglasses, all I could see were water droplets, mud on the windshield of my shades, and trees surrounding me left and right as I cycled on the shoulder of the Trans-Canada Highway. These shades were a game changer. They protected my eyes during bad weather or when trucks slingshot rocks directly towards my eye. Without them, I would crash or be blinded. All I could see was six feet in front of my bike; I was riding in the middle of a cloud. The support van was at a checkpoint every 10 km ahead of me so every 30 minutes or so they would check in to make sure I was okay and redirect me.

At first, I thought the mountains would be the hardest part of cycling across Canada, but it wasn't. The hardest part was the finish. My body felt like Jell-O, and some days I couldn't move my head without having involuntary contractions in my neck, shoulder, and back muscles. I couldn't feel my legs. My thigh was red, three times the normal size, and hot to the touch. My feet were puffy and could barely fit inside my shoes. And my toes, when my socks were off, looked like they went through a cheese grater. I just had to make it to the end.

With only four kilometres left to Africville, this should have been the easiest part of my ride, but it wasn't, it was the hardest. With each pedal, my hamstring was ripping and my calves felt like they would explode. I don't know what I would have done if I hadn't had my support team.

We had a new addition in the support van for our last day . . . my mom. She had watched the journey through social media posts and Instagram stories, but she hopped on a plane to join the crew and celebrate the finish. At the van's final checkpoint, she rolled down the window on the passenger side to take my photo and send it to all her WhatsApp family in a mass message. The glow on her face was all I needed to remember everything we went through and what she did to pave the way for us to have more opportunities.

I was struggling to finish so Bligh grabbed the extra bike from the back of the trailer and rode the final kilometres with me. We took turns trailing behind each other all the way to Africville. Normally four kilometres would take eight minutes to ride, but it took me closer to an hour. As we drifted around the corner of the Africville road, we saw the old rusted "Welcome to Africville" sign—the finish line. We arrived at the corner of the Bedford Basin, a body of water that connected to the Atlantic Ocean. Instead of dipping our front tires into the water to symbolize the finish, I just threw my bike into the ocean and glared at it as it got tossed and flipped in the waves.

After taking the bike out of the water, we gathered to take our team photo standing in the field of Seaview Park, Africville, a National Historic Site of Canada, with the Africville sign and the Africville Museum. With Jarrett, Trey, Addisiane, and Bligh, we held both bikes over our heads to show we had done it as a team. We posed for the photos, surrounded by Addisiane's family, my mom, and my wife and her family, who had all driven or flown to cheer us on as we finished. We were small, but we were still rolling 15 deep.

For me, the best thing about the trip wasn't the ride but the opportunity I had to work with my team. The ride was never about me. The ride was about the people, the communities, and the support team that gave me the ability to turn dreams into reality. It took 60 plus people across Canada, from support teams, donors, and the people who fed us and gave us a place to sleep, to make this work. No position on the team was more valuable than any other. We needed each other and everyone needed to play their part. In the end, we raised a total of $100,000, which covered the trip and the production of the documentary film, with all of the remaining money going to afterschool programs around the City of Toronto through Urban Promise Toronto, which worked in my hood. The money was nice for the hood, but for me it was never about the money. It was about all the stories of the people, which existed with or without the ride. Stories of families, parents, mothers, fathers, children, youth, brothers, and sisters, and the OG grandparents who were still in the trenches like me.

What happened to Africville is happening in the present and will happen in the future, so we had to find a new way to preserve the stories of our community.

The OGs pour some before drinking some, keeping alive the memories of the ones who were lost. Surrounded by thick clouds of weed smoke, we reminisce about the good times. But after cycling coast to coast, the bike taught me a new way to preserve the memories of those around me. To honour those we lost, we have to become the people we needed when we were younger.

PART 2
Transcend

Yesterday I was clever, so I wanted to change the world. Today I am wise, so I am changing myself.

—**Rumi**

When you learn, teach, when you get, give.

—**Maya Angelou**

Become Who You Needed When You Were Younger

There is no greater agony than bearing an untold story inside you.

—Maya Angelou

I *spent 23 years searching for answers until I realized I had to come up with my own.* It's been six months since I was in the middle of New Brunswick, on the shoulder of the Trans-Canada Highway headed east towards Africville. Following the ride, I felt like I was in an empty room filled with darkness. Fitness once brought me joy, but I lost interest in working out. I struggled to get out of bed, and sometimes even struggled to eat like I used to. I didn't know what this was, but I knew my mental health was not okay.

I wanted to scream, but I felt like I was underwater. I tried to achieve myself out of trauma, but it wasn't possible. I was running. I was running from myself, but my past was in my shadow; it was always with me. I did everything I was supposed to do. Cycled across Canada. Fundraised money for afterschool programs across the city. Represented as a voice from my community. Spoke to thousands across Canada. I was no Terry Fox or Rick Hansen. I was just a kid from

Scarborough doing it strictly for the streets. Strictly for hood motivation for people who came up like me.

Just thinking of the ride made me want to go to sleep. Cycling from breakfast to dinner ten plus hours per day in the middle of heat waves was a recipe for disaster. What put me over the edge was trying to keep my eyes open as I spoke to audiences about social injustice across the nation when all my body wanted was to be horizontal. I just wanted to sleep.

Now, I am back in the city streets I was raised in. Mentally, I am not where I started, but physically, I am back where I began. A neighbourhood infested with cops that harassed us on the daily. Schools with teachers that treated us like inmates, had no understanding of the neighbourhood, and never stepped foot in the community across the school yard. Racism took no days off.

I was too busy being oppressed to explain oppression to others. The next year, I would talk to no one. People could easily use Google to find the definition of oppression. The information is there if people care enough to do the work and open a book or YouTube. No one learns from just listening to a talking head. We learn by taking the initiative to find answers, educating ourselves, and doing the work.

The day I got back, I was back to square one. Still losing homies in the streets in underfunded communities, schools, and neighbourhoods we didn't create. And things just seem to be getting worse. I saw the same things play out over and over again over the course of my life, making me feel like each day was a constant state of *déjà vu*. It was too easy to lose hope. I was once too optimistic and naïve, but I started to see the landmines the system set out for us. And yet, they blame us for the conditions of our neighbourhoods. I had to find my way under this system to create a life for myself and my community.

The ride was good for what it was, but I wanted to find a way to help long-term. I knew we needed something more. Technology was rapidly changing the world and we were being left behind. We had limited access to good WIFI and computers outside of school, and this would only get worse before it got better with school and community funding drying up. I wanted to do something for the community, but first I had to figure out my life. It was a mess. I was freshly graduated, couch surfing, and still looking for work as a new teacher.

Each night as I lay in bed, I realized my mental health had been destroyed. My mind was still on auto pilot, replaying my entire childhood on my eyelids as if they were movie screens. All I wanted was sleep.

My whole life, I've heard so many people talking about our hoods even though they had never set foot in them. I just wanted them to take a seat. I wanted to tell a different story, from the inside screaming out. A few years after the ride, I reread the authors and revolutionaries I had come across before the ride began. It was mostly Black women leading the movement, in addition to some Black men who inspired me and helped me understand the moment. My moment, though brief, was something I had to use to take care of the people within arm's reach.

When I started to look outside my block and everything I once knew, the weight on my shoulders started to lighten. I started to research other neighbourhoods and stories, both local and across the country, and began to find inspirational stories of people who were making a real difference in their community. I always got hyped when I found real stories of people from similar circumstances who made it, made something of their life, and came back to help others. I saw in their story or their interviews that these were people who saw the acres of roses that bloomed through concrete . . . roses that were forced to water themselves. My community and communities like mine are royalty in my eyes and I needed to be reminded that there were others who saw their communities the same.

The people I discovered cared about the community and were cosigned by the people within them. All I needed to do was study their stories and identify how they impacted their community and use their model so that I could level up in my community.

One of the greatest barriers we faced growing up in our neighbourhoods was not only the oppression but the erasure that happens after the oppression. Those in power did all they could to erase the social injustices they created in the past and in the present so it was important to fight to be remembered.

Growing up, I loved the library not only for books but for the Internet and computers. Books and Google were my two homies. I would search for anything and everything that could help me understand the world around me and the things my teachers were either unaware of or too scared to talk about. Finding people's stories about Toronto helped me. Just knowing that others from similar hoods made something of their lives and helped their community sparked enough hope within me that I didn't give up on life after the ride. To me, these were the stories that should be required reading and learning in the school classroom.

Butterflies in the Trenches

Yasin Osman

Yasin Osman, aka Yescene, is an award-winning photographer and cartoonist for The New Yorker from Regent Park. In 2015, Yescene founded Shoot For Peace, a photo mentorship program in Regent Park, blending his passions for youth empowerment and the arts. Since then, the program has reached over a hundred youth and has been recognized internationally by Buzzfeed, Upworthy, and CNN. Working with brands such as Nike, Redbull, and The Toronto Raptors, as well as being a frequent photo contributor to Maclean's Magazine and VICE, he has gained thousands of followers through social media platforms, Instagram, and 500px. Through his images, cartoons, and the recently self-published comic book *Grandpa Ali & Friends*, Yescene has told powerful stories of marginalization, culture, and religion. Today, Yescene works with youth in his community while taking photos and making cartoons and continues to inspire people coast to coast as he empowers others to become leaders in their communities.

Dr. Eugenia Duodu

Dr. Eugenia Duodu is the CEO of Visions of Science Network for Learning. Visions of Science is a charitable organization that empowers youth from low-income communities through meaningful engagement in STEM. Eugenia devotes her time to community and global outreach initiatives and is an advocate for education and creating equitable opportunities for youth so they can achieve their full potential. Eugenia Duodu holds both a High Distinction Bachelor of Science in Chemistry & Biology and a PhD in Chemistry from the University of Toronto. Regardless of how far she has come, she still finds time to be grounded in the communities from which she came.

Desmond Cole

Desmond Cole is an award-winning Canadian journalist, bestselling author, radio host, and activist in Toronto. His writing has appeared in the Toronto Star, Toronto Life, The Walrus, NOW Magazine, Ethnic Aisle, Torontoist, BuzzFeed, and the Ottawa Citizen. Cole hosts a weekly radio program on Newstalk 1010. Cole's activism has received national and international attention, specifically on the issues of police carding, racial discrimination, and dismantling systemic racism. Cole was the subject of a 2017 CBC Television documentary, *The Skin We're In*. His first book, also called *The Skin We're In,* was a number one bestseller within a matter of weeks.

Randell Adjei

Randell Adjei is an author, inspirational speaker, arts educator, community activist, and Ontario's first Poet Laureate from the Scarborough community of Malvern. Randell is the founder of one of Toronto's largest and longest running youth-led initiatives, Reaching Intelligent Souls Everywhere (R.I.S.E. Edutainment). Randell is a spoken word practitioner and Edutainer who uses spoken word to empower and create community through Edutainment. He found himself by turning his struggles around to inspire others. As a featured performer on TEDxUTSC he has opened up for Terry Crews, Paul Mooney, Maestro Fresh Wes, and many more. Randell is the recipient of the Identify & Impact Street Level Advocate Awards by the Toronto Youth Cabinet, and the award winner of Best Spoken Word at the Black Canadian Awards. Randell was also named CBC Metro Morning's Torontonian of the Year in 2015 and NOW Magazine's Local Hero. His spoken word is so powerful that he breaks people and rebuilds them within seconds.

Amanda Parris

Born in London, England, and raised on the south side of Jane Street in Toronto, Amanda Parris is a television and radio host who writes a weekly column and is an arts reporter and producer for the CBC (Canadian Broadcasting Corporation). She is the co-founder of the award-winning alternative education organization Lost Lyrics and worked with the Remix Project and the Manifesto Festival. She has spoken about her work at United Nations conferences around the world. Parris completed her Bachelor of Arts Honours degree in Political Science and Women's Studies at York University and her Master of Arts degree in the Sociology of Education at the University of Toronto. Over the course of her career, Amanda has worn many hats, working as an educator, researcher, actress, and community organizer. In 2014, she was named one of Grenada's Top 40 individuals under the age of 40 and in 2018 she was named one of Toronto's Most Inspiring Women by Post-City, a Local Hero of Toronto Film by Now Magazine, and the African Heritage Educators Network (AHEN) named their 2018 Student Arts Award after her.

Anthony Gebrehiwot

Anthony Gebrehiwot, aka TonyTones, is a passionate photographer, community leader, and the founder of XVXY Photo based in Scarborough. To date he has worked with brands such as Nike, Royal Bank of Canada, Vice Canada, Absolute, Hudson's Bay Company, The City of Toronto, LinkedIn, and more. His art and creativity is a process of re-visioning photography as an ongoing conversation of social change between the people he captures and the society that we live in. As a self-taught photographer, Gebrehiwot founded XVXY Photo in 2014, focusing on studio portraiture. His work has been featured in over 30 local and international publications such as the Star, the Globe and Mail, PAPER Magazine, Elle UK, and Yahoo Lifestyle.

Francis Atta

Born in Kumasi, Ghana, Francis Atta immigrated to Toronto with 13 siblings when he was six years old. Growing up in the Jane and Finch community, Francis faced tremendous struggles, dropped out of high school, became homeless, and got into trouble with the law. But he managed to flip his life around, receiving a Bachelor's Degree in Social Work from Ryerson University, an advanced diploma in Child and Youth Studies from George Brown College, and a Master's Degree in Social Work—specializing in mental health and health—from the University of Toronto. Embarking on a career as a child and youth worker, he has become one of the most highly sought-after motivational speakers in Canada through his company K.E.Y.S. (Knowledge and Effort Yield Success), founded in 2010. He learned and reminds others that we have to take the hands that we are dealt and make the most of it. In his book, *The Flip,* you open it one way and it offers inspiration to his younger audience, then flip it and Francis offers advice for parents on how to improve their relationships with their kids, an essential ingredient for them to thrive.

Yusra Khogali

Yusra Khogali is a daughter of a Sudanese diaspora from Regent Park, Toronto. Yusra is a Black feminist multi-disciplinary educator, writer, performance artist, activist, public intellectual, emcee, and grassroots community organizer. She co-founded the Black Lives Matter Toronto movement, which has shifted the current political landscape of Canada by actively working to dismantle all forms of anti-Black racism. In 2019, she announced she was exiting the BLMTO and BLM Global network, but regardless of who she rolls with, she has never wavered from the fight to support Black life. She led the fight against racist systems and systemic violence for many of us in public housing and across the Black and African diaspora, and she is actively fighting for our healing and mental wellness as a people, especially for Black women in the city of Toronto. She also co-founded Black Liberation Collective Canada, a Black student movement that works to create infrastructure for Black students around the globe to build power, using an intersectional lens to eliminate anti-Blackness on campus. She completed her Master's Degree in Social Justice Education at the University of Toronto with a research focus on the Black diaspora and Black African, anti-colonial, transfeminist liberation thought. She kept it one hundred from the jump and fought for Black life on the block, in the city, nationally, and globally.

Growing up, I never read books that took place in Toronto or Scarborough, so when I came across books like *Scarborough* by Catherine Hernandez, *Brother* by David Chariandy, and *Shut Up You're Pretty* by Téa Mutonji as I was finishing university, it changed the game. Their books were confirmation to me that Scarborough was more than worthy to be written about. They put Scarborough on the map and represented it proudly on the world stage. They inspired me to pick up the pen again for the first time in ten years.

David Chariandy

David Chariandy is a bestselling author and university professor who was born in Scarborough. He has a Master's from Carleton University and a PhD from York University and lives in Vancouver where he teaches

English at Simon Fraser University. His debut novel, *Soucouyant,* was published in 2007, but it was his second novel, *Brother,* published in 2017, that won numerous awards, was named the Best Book of 2017 on eight lists, and won the Rogers Writers' Trust Fiction Prize, The Toronto Book Award, and the Ethel Wilson Fiction Prize in 2018. He put himself and Scarborough on the map. *Brother* was the first book I ever read that broke me down but then knitted me back together again, helping me find value in a past that I had become accustomed to running from.

Catherine Hernandez

Catherine Hernandez, who is also from Scarborough, is a theatre practitioner, award-winning author, and the artistic director of b current Performing Arts. Catherine's first full-length fiction book, *Scarborough,* won numerous awards including the Jim Wong-Chu Emerging Writer Award. It was shortlisted for the Toronto Book Award, Edmund White Award for Debut Fiction, Evergreen Forest of Reading Award, Trillium Book Award, and longlisted for Canada Reads. *Scarborough* made the best of 2017 lists for the Globe and Mail, National Post, Quill and Quire, and CBC Books. Catherine was named one of 17 Writers to Watch by CBC Books. Her next power moves were her second children's book, *I Promise,* second novel, *Crosshairs* (2020), third novel, *PSW* (upcoming in 2022), and an upcoming screenplay based on her novel *Scarborough.*

Téa Mutonji

Téa Mutonji is an award-winning writer and poet who was born in Congo-Kinshasa and came to Canada with her family as a child. She did media studies and creative writing at the University of Toronto and now lives and writes in Scarborough. Her debut book *Shut Up You're Pretty,* published in 2019, was the winner of the Trillium Book Award and Edmund White Award for Debut Fiction. It was also a finalist for the Rogers Writers' Trust of Canada Fiction Prize and a *Globe and Mail* Best Book of the Year. Téa paved the way for young Black authors both locally and nationally. She put our city on the map and inspired us, showing us that our voices and our stories deserve to be represented in books.

Mustafa Ahmed

Mustafa Ahmed, aka Mustafa the Poet or Mustafa, was born in Toronto, Ontario, to Sudanese parents and grew up in Regent Park. In Grade 7, he performed an original piece, "A Single Rose," at Nelson Mandela Park Public School. The piece garnered significant attention, earning him high praises at Toronto's Hot Docs Canadian International Documentary Festival in 2009. From a young age, Mustafa created raw and hopeful pieces, inspired by his upbringing in North America's first public housing buildings in Regent Park. During this time, Mustafa was known for writing poems about poverty in both Africa and the Regent Park area. As a member of the Canadian hip hop collective Halal Gang, Mustafa has made appearances in a number of music videos for his crew, including the single "Feel" by Safe, released in October 2016. He went on to co-write and provide background vocals on the song "Attention" on The Weeknd's album *Starboy*. In the same year, Mustafa was appointed to Justin Trudeau's Youth Advisory Council, advising the Prime Minister and the Government of Canada on policies and programs that were important to the council. Mustafa was placed on NOW's list of Toronto musicians to watch in 2017.

In March 2019, Mustafa was asked to collaborate with fashion designer Pierpaolo Piccioli on Valentino's High Fashion Fall/Winter 2019 Collection. He created a series of poems about love for Valentino, and his words and poetry were embroidered on the clothes, shoes, and bags. Vogue described the event as "poetry back in fashion." A year later, in March 2020, Mustafa released his debut single "Stay Alive," which was dedicated to those he'd lost to gun violence. The single was produced by Frank Dukes and James Blake and was praised for including lyrics about resilience, community, and the bleak realities of living on the fringes. The single prompted Complex to include Mustafa on the list of Best New Artists in March 2020. Mustafa's work and dedication to his entire community, family, and friends is a testament to what real community love looks like.

There is something special about all Toronto housing projects, but ever since leaving Regent as a young child, I have been aware that there is something about that community that often gets overlooked. I'm thankful to still be vertical in this life and to see the likes of Yusra, Yescene, Mustafa, and more doing their work for the people who need it most and showcasing the real side of Regent: the people.

Khaleel Seivwright

Khaleel Seivwright is a Toronto-based carpenter who raised over $250,000 on GoFundMe to build durable and insulated tiny shelters for people who are homeless and living outside in the winter across Toronto. Khaleel built approximately 100 tiny shelters that keep an internal temperature around 16 degrees Celsius in -20 degrees Celsius temperatures—with carbon monoxide detectors, one window for light and smoke, and a note to the side that reads, *Anyone is welcome to stay here*—which provided a safer alternative to tent communities dispersed across the city. Due to the shelters being at capacity and the COVID-19 pandemic strain on the health care system, Khaleel not only provided homes and secure lockable storage for those without a place to go, but he saved lives and provided a solution amidst a government who has failed for decades at providing adequate housing, services, and resources for vulnerable populations across the city. As a result of Canada's failure to build adequate affordable housing over the past 20 years, they turned their backs and left people to die when lawmakers could have made a difference. Despite the city of Toronto evicting people from their tiny homes, destroying them at night, and taking legal action to sue him, Khaleel Seivwright is a hero who saw a need and used his skills to provide a solution. In 2020–21, his story was published in *The New York Times,* CBC, CTV, Global News, Blog TO, 680 News, *NOW Magazine*, and Complex. Khaleel Seivwright is the GOAT.

La Mar Taylor

Born and raised in Scarborough, La Mar Taylor is the creative director for The Weeknd and the associated XO brand. He met Abel Tesfaye, The Weeknd, on the first day of his freshman year of high school, and they have been friends ever since. At 17, he dropped out of high school, along with Abel, to pursue a career in the entertainment industry as a director, photographer, and designer. La Mar started his career by taking up creative video projects, album artwork (he was first recognized for creating the cover for The Weeknd's debut mixtape *House of Balloons* in 2011), merchandise, and live shows for The Weeknd. Later, he co-founded the XO record label with The Weeknd and his manager Amir "Cash" Esmailian. With the global impact of his work, he landed on the Forbes 30 Under 30 list for Music in 2017.

In 2018, La Mar co-founded an incubator, HXOUSE, with Ahmed Ishmail. HXOUSE is a Toronto-based and globally focused think-centre serving the community as an incubator and accelerator, helping to foster innovation and opportunity for creative entrepreneurs. A 30,000-square-foot space located near Toronto's waterfront, the facility provides studio rooms and the equipment needed for recording, designing, producing, and more, all at a low cost for young artists. Rather than traditional education, HXOUSE seeks to empower through mentorship and communication, engaging the creative mind through the practice of cross-disciplinary learning, and anchored in the core belief that by thinking outside your discipline, you can learn how to evolve your craft. This was their way of supporting and inspiring Toronto creatives and young entrepreneurs to become giants in their respective fields.

The Weeknd himself needs no introduction. Abel Tesfaye was born in Toronto, Ontario, to Ethiopian immigrants and raised in Scarborough. Tesfaye attended West Hill Collegiate Institute and Birchmount Park Collegiate Institute in Scarborough, from which he did not graduate. With La Mar, he dropped out of high school in 2007 and the rest is history; from Scarborough to performing in the 2021 NFL Superbowl halftime show.

Stephan James, Shamier Anderson, and Sheldon James (The three Scarborough brothers)

Stephan James and Shamier Anderson are award-winning actors and producers born in Scarborough. Stephan is known for the films *Race* (2016), *If Beale Street Could Talk* (2018), and *Selma* (2014). Shamier starred as US Deputy Marshal Xavier Dolls on the television series *Wynonna Earp* and will also star in the upcoming 2021 science fiction thriller film *Stowaway*. As of 2021, the three brothers—Stephan James, Sheldon James, and Shamier Anderson—are founders of Bay Mills Investment Group. This organization offers financial support and mentorship to young Black, Indigenous, and People of Colour (BIPOC) business owners to help them build profitable businesses. They bridge the gap between underrepresented founders and emerging business opportunities with growth capital, network resources, and top-tier mentorship, supporting entrepreneurs across North America. From Bay Mills to the boardroom, they are diversifying the face of entrepreneurship as the first BIPOC venture fund in Canada. They grew up with their mother in the Bay Mills housing projects and went on to become Scarborough legends. They never forgot where they came from and they give back to the city through their initiatives like Bay Mills Investment Group, B.L.A.C.K. Canada (Building A Legacy in Acting, Cinema + Knowledge), and The Black Academy.

The people profiled here are building legacies in real time, and the good work they're doing is just the tip of the iceberg. There are millions of people just like them in every block and hood in Scarborough, Toronto, provincially, nationally, and globally. It's important to keep these stories alive so they aren't erased. Their stories inspire us and show us how to create our own pathways when we're told there aren't any.

Create Something from Nothing

At the end of the day, what you bring to the table will change the field that you're in and no one can bring that except for you.

—Eugenia Duodu

Before I was a sponsored athlete, I was sponsored by the streets. Every time I got credit for any success in my life, I redirected it back to the OGs, homies, elders, and curb servers on the block who held me down and kept me off the streets. When I won, they won. The hustlers helped pay for school and buy sports equipment and they taught me how to read. We faced police raids, food deserts, drive bys, house fires, losing homies, suicides, and getting pushed out of school. And despite everything, we were still surviving. To me that meant something.

The street corner was a classroom that had massive value. There were entrepreneurial skills and activities knitted into the fabric of my hood. I learned start-up culture from local hairstyling services on front porches, mom and pop restaurants operating out of backyards, and T-shirts and mixtapes being sold out of car trunks; from homies that designed clothing lines, built websites as a side hustle, and managed artists. The street corner was a business. The neighbourhood was a start-up organization.

We lived in an environment that demanded creativity to find solutions to new and old problems. And we did this with limited resources and opportunities. I call it Street Corner Innovation. We were always building the plane while we were flying it. We didn't have to have it all figured out before we started. Intelligence could be developed while failing and making mistakes. That's the price to pay to level up.

Street corner innovators exist all around the world. They build creative solutions to help their families and neighbourhoods. Innovators are not just inventors and entrepreneurs, they're also activists, and they didn't necessarily come from the streets, but they took it to the streets.

Street Corner Innovators

Autumn Peltier

At age eight, Autumn Peltier, from the Wiikwemkoong Unceded Territory in northern Ontario, started advocating for clean water for First Nations communities and across Mother Earth. She fights for international environmental justice, for clean water, and for governments to take a stand against climate change with actions instead of lip service. She has earned international acclaim after speaking at the United Nations and the World Economic Forum and confronting Justin Trudeau about the Trans Mountain pipeline. In 2019, she was named the Chief Water Commissioner for the Anishinabek Nation, fighting for safe waterways and drinking water for Indigenous people in Canada and beyond. She broke major ground for Indigenous water rights and is known as a water warrior in Canada, a country where over a hundred Indigenous communities have lived for decades without access to clean water, and as of 2021, still are without access to running water.

William Kamkwamba

William Kamkwamba is an inventor and author from Malawi. In 2001, at age 13, he took inspiration from a library book and built an electricity-producing windmill from junk parts—blue gum trees, bicycle parts, and materials collected in a local scrapyard—to rescue his farming family from a famine. His windmill provided enough electricity and water for his home and his community in rural Malawi. Next, he built solar powered water pumps to supply his village with drinking water along with two additional windmills. His story went viral and got international attention, leading to the release of his autobiography *The Boy Who Harnessed the Wind*, an award-winning feature length film on his life called *William and the Windmill* (2013), and a Netflix film titled *The Boy Who Harnessed the Wind* (2019). William splits his time between the US and Malawi and is currently working full time with the Moving Windmills Project to bring the Moving Windmills Innovation Center to life in Kasungu, Malawi.

Thato Kgatlhanye

Thato Kgatlhanye, born in Mogwase just outside of Rustenburg, South Africa, noticed many of the kids in her community had plastic bags as book bags. In 2013, when Thato was 21, she became the founder and creator of Repurpose Schoolbags, an environmentally friendly schoolbag that uses recycled plastic bags with built-in solar technology and batteries. This technology provides children with up to 12 hours of light to study by. The bags also use reflective materials, making children more visible as they walk to and from school in the dark. She credits the idea to a conversation she had with her mom who grew up studying with candles, which always burned out before she was done.

Ludwick Marishane

Ludwick Marishane is a young South African inventor who, after learning that 2.5 billion people worldwide lack access to water and sanitation, developed a formula for a lotion that could cleanse your body cheaply and easily without the need for water—a bath without water. Soon after, in 2007, he patented his invention, wrote a business plan, and launched his start-up, then called Headbody Industries but now called Dry Bath, the world's first and only odourless antibacterial cleaner that cleans and moisturizes the skin. A lifesaver rather than a tool of convenience, his invention is specifically useful for communities in rural areas that have limited access to water. In recognition of his work, he received the Global Student Entrepreneur of the Year Award in 2011.

Mari Copeny

When she was eight years old, Mari Copeny and her siblings learned not to turn on the water in their home in Flint, Michigan, after news broke that the water was contaminated. Since 2014, people in Flint have been unable to consume city water and are forced to rely on bottled water. This public health crisis continues today. Mari began fundraising and raised over $500,000 and provided clean water, toys, bikes, and other resources to over 25,000 children, helping to ensure families have a healthy life. When the state of Michigan stopped paying for bottled water for Flint in 2019, she switched her focus and partnered with socially responsible companies that provided water filtration systems to communities across the country dealing with toxic water. Now, at 13, Mari is still fighting for the children and families of Flint, Michigan. She is known as "Little Miss Flint."

Kelvin Doe

Kelvin Doe is a Sierra Leonean and self-taught engineer. In 2009, at 13, he taught himself engineering and built his own generator and radio transmitter. At 16, he provided electricity to homes in his communities, which had no constant power supply, by building a battery. This battery was created and designed from acid, soda, and metal parts he found in the trash. Also known as DJ Focus, Kelvin also built his own radio station in Sierra Leone, and he is the founder and president of the Kelvin Doe Foundation, a non-profit organization that is committed to empowering young people in Africa to design innovative solutions to some of the most critical issues in their communities.

Larissa Crawford

Larissa Crawford is a Jamaican-Métis anti-racist and climate justice activist based in Calgary, Alberta. She is the founder of Future Ancestors Services, a youth-led social enterprise focusing on climate justice and equity, working with clients to create more inclusive spaces for diverse people. She served as the youth delegate for Canada and successfully lobbied for Indigenous worldviews and the UN Sustainable Development Goals at the G7 Summit in 2018. She was able to fund her undergraduate degree by representing her university at several global United Nations events, earning $100,000 in scholarships and awards.

Vérone Mankou

Vérone Mankou, born in Pointe-Noire, in the Republic of Congo, is an entrepreneur and inventor that designed the first African touchscreen tablet in 2011 and the first African Smartphone, called Elikia (Hope), in 2012. The goal was to provide quality and innovative smart devices that were affordable in his home country and across the African continent while increasing Internet access nationwide. Today, he continues to train young African entrepreneurs while making his product affordable, hoping to compete with companies like Samsung and Apple.

Arthur Zang

Arthur Zang, a Cameroonian engineer, created Africa's first handheld medical computer tablet. This patented invention, the Cardiopad, is a 25 cm touchscreen tablet that helps diagnose people with heart disease. Since 2014, health workers have used the device to perform electrocardiograms in rural communities. The reports are then sent to doctors wirelessly so they can process, analyze, and interpret the data.

Isra Hirsi

Isra Hirsi is an African American environmental activist and a daughter of the US Congresswoman Ilhan Omar and Ahmed Abdisalan Hirsi. At 12, she was one of the participants in a protest for justice for Jamar Clark, who had been shot by Minneapolis Police and later died in hospital. She became heavily involved in climate activism after joining her high school environment club as a freshman. In January 2019, she coordinated hundreds of student-led strikes across the country and co-founded the US Youth Climate Strike, which is the US branch of the global youth climate change movement.

Vanessa Nakate

Vanessa Nakate is a Ugandan climate justice activist and global change-maker born and raised in Kampala, Uganda. In December 2018, concerned about the unusually high temperatures in her country, she became an activist, earning international headlines and becoming recognized as the founder of the African-based Rise Up Movement and 1MILLION Activist Stories where she shares the experiences of global climate activists, amplifying their voices and helping preserve and protect Mother Earth.

Asidu Abudu

Asidu Abudu is a Ghanaian inventor who developed several mechanical instruments from scratch as a child. He created a machine for grinding fufu (a traditional food across Africa) to relieve women's burden in food preparation, an automated machine for feeding people with disabilities, and a car tracking system that allows you to use your cell phone to stop your car. Inspired by various mechanical designs, he also created a surveillance system via your smartphone with a built-in remote-control system for your car. The app notifies you if someone opens your car door and allows you to view the scene in real time.

Marley Dias

Marley Dias is an African American activist and feminist. In 2005, at 10 years old, she founded the #100Blackgirlbooks—an initiative focused on collecting books that feature Black main characters, not minor or background characters, and donating them to Black girls. She has collected more than ten thousand books and has also published her own book called *Marley Dias Gets it Done and So Can You.*

Evans Wadongo

Kenyan native Evans Wadongo grew up with first-hand knowledge of energy poverty, having come from a rural village with no electricity. He spent days walking long distances to buy a kerosene lamp, which can cause eye problems because of the constant smoke exposure. In 2004, at 18, a dorm room experiment involving LED Christmas lights helped him discover how to build his own environmentally friendly solar lantern that could light up his community. Evans' lantern, which he called MwangaBora—Swahili for "good light"—made from 50 percent recycled material, was widely distributed in Kenya, Malawi, and other countries across the continent. Naming the project Use Solar, Save Lives, he used solar technology as a way to save lives in poor communities like the one he grew up in. This was his way of addressing poor education, climate change, health, and poverty in rural communities.

Abiola Akindele, Zainab Eniola Bello, Adebola Duro-Aina, and Oluwatoyin Faleke

In 2012, Abiola Akindele, Zainab Eniola Bello, Adebola Duro-Aina, and Oluwatoyin Faleke, four girls in high school in Nigeria, became certified inventors and shifted the hearts and minds of the local and international community. In communities that face constant power outages, most households depend on generators as an alternative source of power. But fuel to power generators is scarce. After reading an online story about a family of five that died from carbon monoxide poisoning after inhaling fumes from the generator, the Fantastic Four created their own solution, a urine powered generator that could provide more, safer, and more affordable access to electricity. The invention was born out of their school chemistry lab. With the generator and one litre of urine, households could have six hours of electricity. With their creativity, they used waste products to produce energy. Pee is for power.

Trey Brown

Trey Brown is a 14-year-old CEO of the clothing brand SPERGO, born and raised in the city of Philadelphia. There was a large amount of violence in his community and kids being murdered at a young age, so in January 2018 at the age of 12, he used $178—his birthday money—to start his own clothing company to empower his community and his friends to keep them off the streets and to do something positive in the midst of their circumstances. Along with his mother, Sherell Peterson—the creative director and Chief Financial Officer of SPERGO—Trey started selling t-shirts at local barbers every weekend across the city and two years later grew his clothing company and social presence to a national brand with two stores in Philadelphia. SPERGO is comfortable, unisex, and luxury urban activewear worn by top entertainers and athletes including Ben Simmons, Meek Mill, Diddy, Da Baby, and Lil Durk. In addition to that, he's been featured on CNN and Fox Business, and he had a billboard in New York City's Times Square. Trey is a legend in the city of Philadelphia, a model for making money and reinvesting it into the business, and an inspiration for giving employment opportunities to his family, friends, and community to work at SPERGO.

These innovators are all people who weren't afraid to ask questions and make mistakes. They are the people who inspire me to look at a situation, identify the problem, then stop at nothing to find a solution.

The world is getting more technologically advanced by the day and our public schools aren't designed to keep up with the changes. As the future of work continually changes, I realized it was more important than ever to find a way to prepare for and create the jobs of the future. To secure our bag we have to somehow find a way to remain relevant with new skills. Though we have limited opportunities in STEAM and STEM education (science, technology, engineering, arts, and mathematics), I had to take a leap of faith and figure it out.

At first, STEM and STEAM education looked scary. I was out of the loop, like many in my hood, but I discovered that human brains were actually made to learn about STEM education. It wasn't all about robots, doctors, and computers. It was learning about relevant and real world opportunities and teaching people how to think.

Human brains naturally process information non-linearly instead of in a straight line. Our brains don't think about only one subject. We think across boundaries and make connections between pieces of information to make meaning of ourselves and the world around us. By having separate subjects, schools blur the lines and try to rewire our brain to think in a straight line. But the real world doesn't operate this way. After graduating university, I started to look for more ways to learn outside of school as I needed more STEM skills. I didn't want to be that person who was all talk and no action.

As I reflect on the need for STEM education, I can't help but think about a key piece of Nipsey Hussle's story that often gets overlooked. He co-signed and heavily endorsed a young prodigy from Compton, California, the person who built the mobile app for Hussle's Marathon Clothing store. After seeing this person speak on YouTube, I was inspired to become a self-taught iOS mobile app developer and computer programmer, all at the touch of a button . . . for free.

This legendary individual goes by the name of Iddris Sandu.

Learn a
New Skill

We will always have STEM with us. Some things will drop out of the public eye and will go away, but there will always be science, engineering, and technology. And there will always, always be mathematics.

—Katherine Johnson, *NASA Research Mathematician*

When I moved back to the hood after university, I stumbled across a Twitter post that linked to numerous news articles on Iddris Sandu and his TEDx talk. He was only 21, but the things he was saying about the world, technology, the hood, and the genius that exists on the block were things I had never heard before in my life. I watched every single interview with and speech about him on YouTube. I wanted to understand how he could think on this level and how I could learn from him.

Iddris Sandu

Iddris Sandu was born in Accra, Ghana, and raised in Compton, California, after arriving in the US at age three. Living in a low-income community with limited access to resources and opportunities, Iddris spent a lot of his time in the public library and was fascinated with computer programming and STEM education. After watching Steve Jobs announce the launch of the first iPhone, Iddris was determined to understand how it worked, so he went to the Compton public library for two years straight and made the sacrifices he needed to become a self-taught computer programmer and software engineer. He was so hungry to learn that he only missed two days over the course of those two years. As STEM education resources and opportunities didn't exist for Black and brown youth in his community, the only way he could learn was to teach himself by reading books and using the library computer.

In 2010, after dedicating three years of his life to programming and building software, a designer at Google noticed Iddris reading books at the library and later offered him an internship at Google headquarters. At 13, he was the youngest Google intern in history. Working his way up on numerous projects, the internship gave him first-hand, professional experience with programming.

At that time, at age 15, he went on to create the first mobile app for his high school to help students find their classrooms with a simple step-by-step and turn-by-turn navigation on their smartphones. This mobile application gained national attention and landed him a visit to the White House where he received the Presidential Scholar award from President Barack Obama. Fast forward seven years, at 22, he is a self-taught architectural technologist, computer programmer, and software engineer who has written code and been a paid consultant for Apple, Twitter, Snapchat, Instagram, Facebook, Fenty, Adidas, Uber, Prada, Travis Scott, Rihanna, Migos, Kanye West, Jaden Smith, Elon Musk, and Nipsey Hussle.

In 2019, after being smart with his money, Iddris announced that he purchased nine acres of land in Accra, Ghana, with plans to build a state-of-the-art STEM educational hub with a focus on mental wellness. Inspired by the life and work of his friend Nipsey Hussle, his goal was to help youth like him learn about STEM education and digital technology and make Ghana known as the tech coast. He was off to a good start after starting two companies, ethosDNA and spatiaLABS, a tech company building interactive mixed reality experiences and the future of spatial computing.

Nipsey Hussle co-signed Iddris and labelled him the future of tech and leader of the new generation for his revolutionary view of the world. Iddris' mission was to use STEM and hip hop culture to inspire communities to become creators rather than consumers as the big money is out there for people who create things with technology. I started to see that there was money in creating technology or online content. Iddris and Nipsey developed a deep friendship over the last few years of Nipsey's time on earth and bonded over books. They not only read books on technology, STEM education, sales, marketing, business, entrepreneurship, finances, taxes, mental health, real estate ownership, and corporations, they also read books to discover more about who they were as Black people and the Black experience in the US. They found value and beauty in their African roots and across the diaspora. They read books like *Message to the Blackman in America* by Elijah Muhammad, *Three Magic Words* by U. S. Andersen, *Blood in My Eye* by George L. Jackson, *The 22 Immutable Laws of Marketing* by Al Ries and Jack Trout, *The Fire Next Time* by James Baldwin, *The Invisible Man* by Ralph Ellison, *Malcolm X Talks to Young People* and *Power Vs. Force* by David R. Hawkins, my favourite, *The Spook Who Sat by the Door* by Sam Greenlee, and all of Malcolm Gladwell's books.

Learning from Nipsey and Iddris, it became even more clear to me that I couldn't wait for change to come from people in power or outside of my community. Throughout history, change came from the people who took it to the streets. These were people who realized the revolutionary power they had. I needed to find a way to do it for myself, and if I was struggling, I needed to reach out to others around the community who looked out for us to help guide me along the way.

Iddris was working on a new technology for Uber's first self-driving car at the local Starbucks when Nipsey Hussle, realizing that he was creating something new, approached him. Nipsey offered him the chance to work side-by-side with him to turn his Marathon Clothing store into the first ever "smart store." Iddris designed an augmented reality mobile app that brought the store to life for customers. Customers would use their smartphone to scan tags in the store that would then display interactive visual and audio experiences that were exclusive content, only experienced in the store at Crenshaw and Slauson in South Central LA. This improved the retail shopping experience by using tech as a tool to increase customer interaction with the brand and community. The number one thing I learned from Iddris was his willingness to dedicate his life to learning, sharing knowledge openly with others, and freely teaching people from the hood about STEM and tech.

To me, the stereotypical person in a STEM career was some old white dude in a black and white photo that never saw sunlight and only had computers as friends. Iddris changed that image for me. With long hair, body tattoos, and a love of Afrobeats, dancehall, reggae, and hip hop culture, his story always hit different for me. As a Black kid wearing a hoodie and dreads with a love for the culture, he changed what it meant to be a techie and computer programmer. He shifted the narrative and made STEM education and tech cool.

Albert Einstein was super cool and did amazing things for the world of science, but Iddris doing what he did from the mud was legendary. Coming up as a kid, I heard about Compton through my love of N.W.A, Eazy-E, Dr. Dre, Kendrick Lamar, Roddy Rich, The Game, Serena and Venus Williams, and former Toronto Raptor DeMar DeRozan. So when I heard Iddris' story, I had to find out more.

One of the most pivotal moments of his childhood happened in the public library when a white student who lived in a wealthier neighbourhood came up to Iddris, took the computer programming book out of his hands, and said, "This book is not for people like you." He could have stopped learning after this encounter, but he didn't. Iddris refocused himself and kept on his mission to get access to information that was not easily accessible in his neighbourhood. Low-income communities,

Black and brown communities, have the talent, but opportunities for STEM education is not universal. It's the 2020s and we still live in hoods that don't have access to computers, technology, and good WIFI. In many ways, we were left behind, but Iddris knew we didn't need everything to start. Just one computer, the Internet, and some books would be a good starting point to learn from others and teach ourselves things we were not getting from school. Just like him.

Through his inspiration, I saw how STEM and hip hop have natural connections and work with one another. When I thought of STEM and hip hop, I thought of both of them as entrepreneurial, like a start-up organization. By definition a start-up is an organization that creates a new product or service under uncertain conditions. Hip hop to me was a start-up. Kids didn't care what resources or opportunities they had or didn't have, they just chose to make art wherever and however they could. I saw hip hop as a tool. I saw technology as a tool. Iddris showed people like me that it is possible to get a tech and STEM education; that we could use the arts and things like hip hop as a bridge to learn about STEM and STEAM education.

Gaps in Technology

When Snapchat first launched its facial recognition technology, they had a boatload of errors, most notably, they could not detect Black faces on their mobile app. With a bit more digging, I found that the computer programmers behind the technology created algorithms and lines of code with clear blind spots. Many early detection technologies like bathroom sensors for soaps, taps, and hand dryers, and most dangerously, self-driving cars had similar blind spots. It was discovered during test simulations that self-driving cars were able to detect white people in front of the car but could not detect Black people. The truth is that technology is a tool and cannot be biased, but the people who program the technology can be. In the world of programming, this is called algorithmic bias.

As I write this, the majority of the programmers behind the most well-known social media app companies in North America are 18–35-year-old white males. Whether intentional or not, this was a massive screw up that negatively impacted Black people. I started to see that if these designs continued for the future, more advanced facial recognition software that governments use to surveil the population will also be inherently flawed. We need more diverse populations running companies, creating tech, and writing code. With individuals like Iddris, who are more diverse, not only in race but in life experiences, tech could better represent the diverse world we live in, solve world issues, and build more creative businesses.

These gaps in technology were the proof I needed to see the value that low-income and Black communities could bring to solving technological issues around the world. Inspired by this discovery, I made my transition from a STEM education advocate to a person who practised by doing, just as Iddris said. All I needed was a computer and a good Internet connection to start up.

⊰•❈•⊱

I hadn't been back to the Toronto Public Library since I was a kid because I had too many late fees. Being poor is expensive. In my 20s, I got my new library card and asked the librarian what access the card gave me to free online learning. I found out that many libraries across North America have partnerships with businesses that provide online learning platforms free with a library card. Looking through all the courses and online websites available, I saw high quality courses in any and every subject I could think of including but not limited to 3D animation, audio and music, business, computer science, IT, education, sales and marketing, photography, video, app development, and website development.

The library hooked me up with Lynda.com, which is now LinkedIn learning, and similar platforms I could use to teach myself iOS mobile app development. This was how I made my own augmented reality mobile app from scratch. All the courses I took provided a certificate of completion and, three hundred plus hours of online learning later, I tested Iddris' thesis and it worked. All I needed was a computer, some good WIFI, and the discipline to stick with it for a few months. I followed some of the top iOS mobile app developers on YouTube, like *CodeWithChris* and *Lets Build That App,* who offer people from beginner to expert free step-by-step tutorials on how to build apps. At the touch of a button, I learned app development. I got thousands of dollars of educational gems for zero dollars.

With a deep search on Google, I discovered businesses were charging anywhere from $40,000 to $60,000 Canadian to create the augmented reality mobile app I wanted. I didn't have that kind of money to blow so I became a self-taught app developer and created it myself. As a new iOS developer and STEM elementary teacher I gained more tools online than I ever had in school. These are skills I can now use to make money in just a few months or so of doing the right online courses. In-person learning has major advantages and online learning is not for everyone, but once I figured out how to use my critical thinking and analytical skills online, I learned enough on the topic to bring that knowledge back to my people.

Now I could use my skill not only to build apps as a side hustle, but I could teach the younger ones in grade school and high school a skill they could use to make money.

It was crazy that at the touch of a button I could freely learn an in-demand skill that I could later monetize. In my mind, the difference between hustling to survive and finding a new hustle to level up were two sides of the same coin. Same hustle, different muscle. Self-education.

Looking up salaries in technology really showed me the financial possibilities of jobs in the STEM field, specifically computer programming. iOS developers—people who create mobile apps for Apple's iOS operating system—often have significantly higher starting salaries than teachers. According to the reported salaries on Indeed, Glassdoor, and PayScale, the average base salary for iOS developers, as of August 2020, was $82,515.67 per year in Canada and $103,602 in the US. We couldn't get this kind of money hustling in the streets as a curb server. One technology job could bring in four to ten times more money than an entire household in my hood. In the STEM field, there are thousands of different jobs and businesses to create. Every year, new jobs are being created. Mobile app development was just one of them.

Developers are being paid big money to build apps or take on other software engineering roles. The future is tech. Money is good. People have jobs that they can easily work from home. This inspired me and some of the youngins to learn new skills. Growing up, on the corner, we were taught the larger the risk, the bigger the paycheque, but STEM and entrepreneurship don't follow the same rules. With some online business, social media, or tech jobs, people can do this from home and never step foot on the corner. In some ways, now the smaller risk on my life could be the biggest paycheque. With technology, teachers were no longer the gatekeepers of knowledge. The world was at our fingertips.

The two most used operating systems for smartphones worldwide are Apple iOS and Google Android. Both have their own mobile app stores, which creates a demand for iOS and Android app developers. The great thing about learning an object-oriented programming language to become an app developer is that when you learn one programming language, it's easy to pick up another. All these languages are in the same family and follow the same concepts, the only difference is how it's written. Many developers go to college or university for a STEM-related or computer science degree or do an accelerated boot camp certificate program in app development. But a large number of developers are also self-taught and learn how to code on their own. They are able to build a resume of projects as good as the graduates and get the same jobs. The key was to find out what new jobs would be created and learn the skills needed for them.

Across the globe, STEM jobs are increasing at a faster rate than non-STEM jobs. As a result, there are millions of job vacancies around the world and not enough people with the necessary skills to fill them. These numbers only increased during the COVID-19 pandemic and will continue to increase beyond the year 2030. While everything was locked down and physical locations were closed, digital technology and online businesses were still open and making loads of profit.

As the majority of public schools across North America are still preparing kids for the 1950s instead of the 2030s and beyond, I had to figure out how to bring my STEM skills to my people and give them opportunities we didn't have on the block. I needed to figure out how to bring it in a way that would help us secure the bag without having to risk our lives or our freedom.

The original purpose of the public school system was to prepare people to work in factories. But that world no longer exists. We are living in a world with facial recognition technology, artificial intelligence, machine learning, STEM, people working from home, start-up organizations, online businesses, social media, and computers replacing human jobs. Schools in the hood are not preparing us for this new world, and I had to do something about it. I was not interested in standing on the sidelines.

Just like Iddris, there was Antoine Patton (Antoine.digital). He is an African American who learned how to code in prison while serving an eight-year sentence. Once free, he taught his daughter how to code, and now he runs his own technology company with his family. His company teaches people around the world, particularly Black communities, how to code.

Black people exist in STEM in many ways, but I noticed that our contributions—when we have the opportunity to make contributions—aren't recorded or widely acknowledged, and this is true for the United States, Canada, countries around Europe, and anywhere Black people live. After cycling across Canada and speaking to teachers, students, and principals, I noticed that there are limited opportunities in STEM for housing projects here, just like in the United States. With under-funded schools and community programs, I started to see that the lack of access was also systemic. It wasn't that we weren't interested in this type of education. We were excluded.

STEM and technology has the opportunity to either bridge the gap between the rich and poor or make the gap bigger than it's ever been. If we need to prepare for the jobs of the future but are not being taught what we need in school, we have to find a way to learn on our own.

Showing people how to fish and giving them fishing rods or the tools to make fishing rods is what we need. Our neighbourhoods don't lack talent, they lack opportunity. There are many similarities in STEM and entrepreneurship on the street corner. Whether it was Iddris from Compton via Ghana or Dr. Eugenia Duodu from Etobicoke in Toronto, the goal was the same: empower the people to create opportunities for themselves and expose communities to new opportunities. All across the world, people chose self-education and reading books to help them overcome the odds. The future is literally in our hands. The world is literally at our fingertips. All we need to do is find a way to tap in.

We didn't have to have a STEM career or professional computer programmer job. I knew just having a basic understanding of STEM education could help people become better leaders and thinkers in any job or business they wanted in the present or the future.

Anything that can go digital will go digital. Anything that can be automated will be automated. Knowing this, I didn't want others like me to get left behind. Learning a new STEM skill to teach others was one step towards helping my block, but I still had to figure out a way to be accessible to the hood if anyone needed help.

After cycling across Canada, my perspective began to shift and I looked at my life without all the titles and materials I had gained over the years. I thought breaking the cycle of poverty was all about making it out of the hood, but now I saw success differently. Success for me wasn't about making it out of the hood, it was about making my life and my community better.

Success Isn't Making It Out, It's Making Your Life Better

> *I tell my students, "When you get these jobs that you have been so brilliantly trained for, just remember that your real job is that if you are free, you need to free somebody else. If you have some power, then your job is to empower somebody else."*
>
> —Toni Morrison

If public schools won't teach us what we need to know to improve our circumstances and take care of our families long-term, we somehow have to find a way to get the information, teach ourselves, and find those who will support us as we learn. Outside of school and learning from others, there are only two ways to learn what we need to know about life: reading and self-education.

In 2020, I was still in the hood where I grew up in Scarborough, but it was frozen in time. Not much had changed other than the people who lived there. Some of the new families on the block had come from other neighbourhoods because of gentrification so there were a lot of new faces. Whenever I had the time, I would come back and visit to see the kids and the community leaders who were still here. It always felt good to be back, but this time was different.

"Yoooooooooooooo Curtis!"

As I turned around on my bike to follow the sounds, I saw two kids I could not identify in the distance racing towards me on their bicycles. Once they got closer, I recognized one of them.

"What's good lil homies?" I echoed down Cataraqui, the main street I grew up hustling on.

"I wanna make some money. Give me some free game," the girl mumbles while doing a wheelie and circling me on her BMX.

I knew her, but not the kid she was with. He was new on the block. I heard his family had been promised a place in Regent Park but ended up here against their will instead. As he looked me up and down, he screwed up his face and squinted, the sunlight blinding his eyes.

"You that guy who rode across Canada for the block?" he said with a poker face.

"Maybe, maybe not. Depends who's asking."

"Ya that's him. He's always on that humble wave but he's the Black Terry Fox."

Rolling up to me on his bike, he leaned forward with his right hand, we slapped palms, and slid our hands to a closed fist.

"Mad respect," he whispered as they both retreated up the street, back to the ball court.

I was nowhere close to Terry Fox's life or impact, but I understood the heart of what they were saying.

It had been a few years since the ride, and I knew the kids needed more than just inspiration. They needed tools. They wanted to make money and learn new skills, and I wanted to give them the books and tools we didn't have in the hood but I now had in my possession. Books that helped me along the way. Just like them, we never needed to be told what to do. We just needed more options and opportunities to choose from. A major part of the solution was skill sharing, when people come together and share what they know with each other without asking for anything in return. Skill sharing is teaching people different skills so they can create their own opportunities and make money to take care of themselves and their family. Instead of drug dealing, I've seen kids start online businesses building websites and apps, a skill they learned for free and later used to earn money. Instead of only working a minimum wage part-time job, youth learned how to set up a small business and start their own hair salons as a side hustle. Instead of only working a full-time 9 to 5 job, some people left the curb serving to start their own speaking businesses. Once they got going, they earned more in an hour of speaking than a whole month of selling drugs. We need our own financial literacy and entrepreneurial coach, someone who grew up just like the kids, teaching them how to manage money, save, invest, and build long-term wealth. Instead of facing racism in school without help, we need community workers educating us on the school to prison pipeline, giving us tools and strategies to navigate the system. These investments may not seem like much, but for many of us, it's enough to empower us to speak up for ourselves so we don't get bullied by the teachers, principals, and guidance counsellors who do everything in their power to kick us out of school. Skill sharing is a great cheat code in life. The best skill sharing comes from the people who look like us and know the struggle.

Hopping on my bike, I rode around with the kids on the block. To them I was just cruising, but to me, I was starting to remember the losses we took and the wins we celebrated. Seeing the parking lots outside the ball court, I remembered the smile on Blue Boy's face, the block parties and cookouts that kept the community together, the bleacher reactions when someone got dunked on at 52 or got an "and one," the Guinness World Record pop a wheelies, roller skating up and down the sidewalk with no breaks, and the youth breaking the speed limit with their two-foot tall mini motorcycles. I remembered the girls double dutchin' and drawing hopscotch in the middle of the street; the hustlers cracking jokes, freestyling, and storytelling on the corner by the green electrical box; the legendary arguments over a missed foul call; and the slap of Dominoes loud enough to break the wooden table. I remember the OG grandparents, moms, and dads dancing at community BBQs, eating the best Caribbean foods, and dying of laughter until the sun woke up. I could never forget the competing melanin-rich music, blaring so loud that you thought it was a competition to see who could make the speakers explode the fastest.

Sitting on the steps of the ball court at 52 Cataraqui 12 years ago, I never thought I would do anything with my life. At the time, I couldn't see the future because the present was already too much to handle. I once thought breaking the cycle of poverty was all about making it out of the hood because, as kids, we were told the only goal was to make it out and away from the trauma, pain, and violence. Now I saw success differently. Now I knew that we weren't the ones who underfunded the neighbourhoods and schools; we didn't create the conditions for the pain. Success for me wasn't about making it out of the hood, it was about making my life and community better.

As a kid, I thought I was searching for success. In the end, I was searching for myself. Success to me wasn't all about changing postal codes. Success was being at peace with myself and finding ways to support myself financially, take care of my mental health, provide for my family, and do my part in improving the neighbourhood. Success reminded me of Dre, who went to prison for a couple decades but later became an advocate for mental health and well-being, financial literacy, and entrepreneurship . . . all from behind bars. Though he was no longer with us on the outside, he taught us that a key to success was finding new ways to make money when we ran out of ideas.

People in the hood were walking talking start-up organizations. I've seen my homie Devante take off with his love for storytelling through video and photography, landing gigs with Jordan, Nike, and more. I saw a homegirl start her own makeup line and become a YouTuber. I saw drug dealers turn their lives around, get therapy for their mental illness, and later get into real estate and starting a family business. I've seen people become technology entrepreneurs, building websites and mobile apps and receiving more money than they ever saw before. Throughout my neighbourhood, I saw numerous front porch hair salons and restaurants operating out of people's backyards. We were start-up founders and CEOs from the time we were born. We just didn't have a name for it other than hustling. You could start a business on the street corner, out of the trunk, or off the curb which gave us transferable skills and lessons that we learned to get legit and make a name for ourselves. We were already creating a lot from limited resources. I could only imagine what would be possible if we had more tools to work with and new skills to share.

Society gave us a script to follow based on our postal code and skin colour, but we ripped that stuff up and made a script of our own.

My story has helped many people, but at the same time, some of my stories have also pissed some people off. I do not speak for all hoods across the city and country. I don't represent all of the past, present, and future Black people. I am just a kid from Scarborough who started on the corner. I just took the mic back from the so-called experts with their drone-like perspectives of our hoods, who've never stepped foot in our neighbourhoods. I needed to speak for myself.

There is always danger in a single story. My story is just a snippet, frozen in time. In the streets, our lives may have many overlapping stories, but each story speaks for itself. All stories are needed to paint the full picture of what is happening to the lives of those in housing projects across the country. The neighbourhood I grew up in is a different community today. The next generation has a voice to speak for themselves and write their own story, they don't need others to write it for them. To me, the trenches were any life circumstances we couldn't control but had to live with until we figured out a better way. Many things happened around us and to us, but they were all a part of moulding us into who we are.

My start in life wasn't the greatest. All I can do is control how I finish. Looking back on my life, I wouldn't change a thing.

Growing up, all I wanted was to feel like I had the power to choose what I wanted. I didn't want to be limited or told what to do with my life.

It's been a long time since I was hustling on the corner, and I am now an entrepreneur as a keynote speaker, an activist, app developer, and computer programmer. I finally have other skills to share. No matter where I go or what I do in the future, I will still be accessible to those in my ends in Scarborough and blocks like it around the city. Whether it was sharing information or educating others about money, starting a business, learning about technology, or finding someone to talk to about mental health, I was the new plug on the block that could connect people to the services they needed. I didn't have much, but I decided to use stories of people who became the change they were looking for, people who used books and self-education to improve their lives outside of the school classroom. Nipsey Hussle was just one of them.

In our neighbourhood, we didn't need social media photo ops, superficial change, or broken promises from politicians looking for more campaign votes for the election. We needed people around us who understood the community, who saw our community as "we" and not "them." We needed a community centre that didn't shut their doors on us kids at 4:00 p.m. on weekdays. We needed a community centre that actually helped the youth and families in the neighbourhood it was located in instead of only providing services to external communities. We needed direct services. We needed donations to organizations to come to those who needed them most instead of filling the pockets of the people who ran the charities and non-profits.

We were used to the programs coming for two years then disappearing because the funding dried up. We needed community-based opportunities that could help us secure the moneybag long-term. We needed a way to take care of our families today, tomorrow, and for the future. Currently, the moneybag is in business, entrepreneurship, arts, finances, digital technology, and STEM fields. But as with many hoods, these educational opportunities aren't available on my block and aren't taught in school in a way that empowers us financially. We wanted programs that taught us how to understand money, manage money, and build businesses that were sustainable so we could make a life for ourselves and our family. We needed tools and community-based opportunities that could help us long-term. We needed opportunities that equipped us for the future and gave us the skills to jump over the barriers. With sustainable funding, I knew there could be more opportunities to teach the block long-term.

I know there's no blanket solution for all societal issues, but I also know it's important to give us the tools to create for ourselves. We didn't want more community programs just for the sake of increasing the number of services. We needed quality over quantity. What we truly needed on my block was the right long-term programs, tailor-made for the community. It wasn't about dropping off a suitcase of money in the hood. It was about rethinking everything about how cities were designed and what it meant to provide long-term, community-based, and community-led opportunities. Opportunities that give those of us who need it the most the skills and tools to break the cycle and improve our lives and communities mentally, physically, socially, spiritually, financially, and economically. In the end, I started to see that we weren't going to get those opportunities from school or the government; somehow we would have to do it for ourselves instead.

Black, Indigenous, and low-income youth are innately genius with unmatched creativity. We just need the right platforms to showcase it. This is not only true for the youth who are on track to college or university, it's also true for the youth in prison, detention centres, alternative schools, and last chance education facilities. It's true for the curb servers and youth with tattoos and sneakers. All of us have our own genius, and we don't need to sacrifice our identity to be successful.

With the right people around us, people who care about our livelihood, and the right opportunities, we can showcase our creativity on other platforms. For my block, I wanted kids to know we could be from the hood and intelligent all at the same time. We don't have to separate the two; they are all interconnected.

In the end, we found a way to survive when people outside of our neighbourhoods told us we wouldn't make it to 25. Despite the odds, we were still alive and still breathing, so to me that had to mean something. I knew they were wrong about us and our communities. I always knew we were the butterflies and we were living in the trenches.

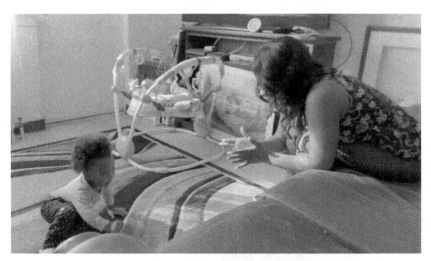

Resources for Download

Reading group and educator guides for middle school, high school, college, university, and book clubs are available for download at: www.CurtisCarmichael.ca

Acknowledgements

This book would not be possible without the amazing people in my corner who showed me love and endless support throughout the roller coaster ride of balancing life, writing, and the processing I needed to do. For helping me bring this book from an idea all the way to print, I would like to thank my wife Kassandra Marling, and my writing coach Jenna Tenn-Yuk. I would like to thank editors Adebe DeRango-Adem, Todd Hunter, Candida Hadley, Lisa Frenette, Adrian So, Amanda Lee, Adrianna Marling, Lewelin Polanco, and Karen Milner for guiding me from start to finish. For creating the design for the book mobile app, special thanks to our Montreal connect Winnie Abodo Alinga. For capturing my community and neighbourhood story in black and white and in colour, shout out to my Scarborough homies, Anthony Gebrehiwot aka TonyTones of XVXY Photo, Devante Thomas, Jarrett Murray for all the ride across Canada photos and videos, and the director and producer of the animated book trailer JonJon, who were major keys in telling the story.

For the community of people that helped support the early stages of the book, special thanks to Donna Carter, Tania Camuti, Risa Tsiotsikas, Adrianna Marling, Addisiane Freeland, Mr. Vasile Radu, Rachael Wallace, Shannon McKinley, James Codd, Matthew Webster, Emilio Frometa, Kassandra Marling, Jason Shamatutu, Tamara

Twumwah-Ofori, Jessica Pozzulo, Synge Chen, Peter Bolton, Bligh Williams, Joshua Greenbaum, and Nicholas Maraj. Special shout out to our researcher Matthew Campbell-Williams and Canadian legend Yusra Khogali whose activism and deep love for the community inspired me and my block. Thanks for paving the way and setting the standard. For seeing potential in the Ride for Promise before it began and creating the documentary to capture it, endless love and special thanks to the legendary Sherien Barsoum and Taza Media Inc. Thanks for giving me the platform to speak truth and taking the story to the screen. For creatively capturing the cycling journey, special thanks to the creative camera and editing crew including Alan Poon, Jarrett Murray, Cameron Hilts, Keyon Slowly, Justin Lovell, Michael Del Monte, James Blokland, Ben Fox, and the entire team that made it possible.

For believing in the Ride for Promise vision and providing the resources to make the ride across Canada possible, special thanks to John McAuley, Ralph Moulton, Deborah and Brian Marling, Peter Deborowski, Urban Promise Toronto (Tim Hill, Lynda and Peter Kentie), Stephen Devlin, Gordon Kentie, Paul Devries, Leanna and Gregg Filmon, Deborah and Dave Guebert, Curtis Sangster, Katherine Savage, all our hosts and accommodations across Canada in each city, and to Dixie Ford for the support van to make the journey smoother and more lavish. Special thanks to my cycling coaches Neil and Cameron Mitchell for pushing me beyond my limits to prepare. Special shout out to the support van crew for supporting me and keeping me safe, well fed, hydrated, and focused when I wanted to quit during the cycle from British Columbia to Nova Scotia: to Trey O'Connor, Bligh Williams, Addisiane Freeland, Cameron Pederson, and Mr. Worldwide himself, our legendary videographer, Jarrett Murray. It wouldn't have been possible without all of you. For giving me a space to finish writing and editing, thanks to A Different Booklist, Staples Studio, Artscape Daniels Launchpad, ildsjel collective, the Marlings, and my mom's living room floor.

For keeping me ten toes down in life and reminding me to never forget where I came from, I would like to shout out to my family, my tens toes down to Susan Millette, Julius Naredo, Ayesha Madden, Kelly

Stouffer, Emilio Frometa, Sam Doucette, Yann Dika, the xXtrovert crew, Solocuts, Marlon Allen, Robert Fukumoto, and all the mandem from Scarborough that held me down, and all the amazing kids, youth, and families from Cataraqui still holding it down. For inspiring me to dream bigger and keep working for the people, shout out to Louis March (ZGVM), mama dukes, Keisha, Michael Clemons, Trey O'Connor, Ayesha Madden, Keyon Slowly, Bligh Williams, Rob Bagg, Shad, Orlando Bowen, Skye Bowen, Salman Mohamed, Shahriyar Patwary, Solo Cuts Studios, E, Mide Akerewusi, Milton Irving, Eugene Williams, Richard Amardi, Todd Hunter, Jordan Thoms, Waveney Job, my Queen's Football Homies (receiveru, playmakers, and the land wolf sharks), all the youth from my neighbourhood Block 13, and Jeff Chan for all the Queen's football photos. For showing the world that Scarborough stories were worth writing about, thank you to Adrian De Leon, Natasha Ramoutar, Téa Mutonji, Catherine Hernandez, and David Chariandy who gave me inspiration to pick up the pen and keep writing at times when I wanted to quit. For teaching me the importance of entrepreneurship, family, and sticking to my word, I would like to thank my brothers, block homies, and the street corner in Scarborough that raised me. For bringing me into this world, giving me a reason to live, and showing me the embodiment of real love, I am and forever will be the person I am today because of my mother, Holly Carmichael. Lastly, for believing in me and my radical moon shots and big dreams at times when things did not make any sense, I would like to thank my wife, my partner in crime, Kassandra Marling, who embodies the true meaning of what it is to be a light and a creative soul. Thank you for being the most caring person I know, keeping me grounded, and being the key to success in any and everything. There are not enough pages in this book to say how great and special you are. Much love and respect. I love you.

Special shout out to the big bros on the block who gave me the love for learning and taught me to get smarter by reading so I could get richer in all areas in my life, not just in the money category. Full circle.

In the words of the Toronto legend Stephan James: Scarborough to the world!

Butterflies in the Trenches

Playlist

1. "Dedication," Nipsey Hussle ft. Kendrick Lamar
2. "Changes," Tupac
3. "Cold Summer," Fabolous
4. "Stay Alive," Mustafa
5. "Black Habits I," D Smoke
6. "What It Feels Like," Nipsey Hussle, JAY-Z
7. "The Fool Pt 1 (Get it Got it Good)," Shad
8. "Thirteen," Haviah Mighty
9. "It Ain't Hard to Tell," Nas
10. "War Baby," Roddy Ricch
11. "Snowchild," The Weeknd
12. "Mortal Man," Kendrick Lamar
13. "Lowered the Heights," John River
14. "Dodging the Devil," Mereba
15. "Handsome," Dave East
16. "PTSD," G Herbo ft. Chance the Rapper, Juice WRLD, & Lil Uzi Vert
17. "Ali," Mustafa
18. "Count On You," Nipsey Hussle ft. Spider Loc & Bino Rideaux
19. "4 Your Eyes Only," J. Cole
20. "Catch the Sun," Lil Baby

21. "Ye," Burna Boy
22. "Trauma," Meek Mill
23. "Crenshaw and Slauson (True Story)," Nipsey Hussle
24. "Dear Mama," Tupac
25. "Real Shit," J. Stone
26. "Effortless," Nipsey Hussle ft. Bino Rideaux
27. "All The Stars," Kendrick Lamar, SZA
28. "Wishing Well," Juice WRLD
29. "For the Win," Friyie
30. "Monsters You Made," Burna Boy ft. Chris Martin
31. "Quicksand," Morray
32. "What More Can I Say," GI JOE OMG FT. J Black
33. "Dreamland," Morray
34. "River," Leon Bridges
35. "Blue Laces 2," Nipsey Hussle
36. "Keep Ya Head Up," Tupac
37. "Before I Go," John River
38. "Nosetalgia," Pusha T ft. Kendrick Lamar
39. "Lost Souls," H.E.R.
40. "Good Kid," Kendrick Lamar
41. "Headshots," Tobe Nwigwe ft. D Smoke
42. "Agape," Nicholas Britell
43. "Juicy," The Notorious B.I.G.
44. "Jungle," H.E.R.
45. "Mo Money Mo Problems," The Notorious B.I.G.
46. "Focus," H.E.R.
47. "Starboy," The Weeknd
48. "Love," Nipsey Hussle
49. "Bigger Than Life," Nipsey Hussle
50. "PTSD," Dreamville ft. Omen, Mereba, Deante' Hitchcock, & St. Beauty
51. "Hope City II," John River
52. "If I Ruled the World," Nas, Lauryn Hill
53. "That's How I Knew," Nipsey Hussle
54. "Toast," Koffee
55. "Oodles and Noodles," Meek Mill
56. "Die Young," Roddy Ricch
57. "High for Hours," J. Cole
58. "The Story of OJ," JAY-Z

59. "Make It Home," Tobe Nwigwe
60. "Loaded Bases," Nipsey Hussle ft. CeeLo Green
61. "Killa," Nipsey Hussle
62. "50 Niggaz," Nipsey Hussle
63. "Sing About Me/Dying of Thirst," Kendrick Lamar
64. "Deep Reverence," Big Sean ft. Nipsey Hussle
65. "Real Big," Nipsey Hussle
66. "Real Life," Burna Boy ft. Stormzy
67. "Magic," Shad
68. "Overtime," Nipsey Hussle
69. "1985," J. Cole
70. "Nas is Like," Nas
71. "The Other Side of America," Meek Mill
72. "HiiPower," Kendrick Lamar
73. "Keep Shining," Shad
74. "Harder Than My Demons," Big Sean
75. "Bigger," Jay Wyse
76. "Don't Take Days Off," Nipsey Hussle ft. Dubb & Tai Phillips
77. "Just a Man," K-Drama
78. "Made Me Everything," TOBi
79. "The Weather," Nipsey Hussle ft. Rick Ross & Cuzzy Capone
80. "Face The World," Nipsey Hussle
81. "Mark My Words," Nipsey Hussle ft. Rick Ross
82. "Destiny," Burna Boy
83. "THS," Jon Hope ft. Israel Wusu
84. "Slow Up," Jacob Banks
85. "My God," Jon Hope ft. Ceez, Israel Wusu
86. "The Blacker The Berry," Kendrick Lamar
87. "Unholy War," Jacob Banks
88. "Brother (Watching)," Shad
89. "Where I'm From," JAY-Z
90. "Alright," Kendrick Lamar
91. "Outro," Nipsey Hussle
92. "Lay Me Bare," Stormzy
93. "City Blues (Remix)," TOBi ft. The Game
94. "Skurr," Nipsey Hussle ft. Bino Rideaux
95. Earn Your Leisure Podcast

CURTIS CARMICHAEL is an award-winning social entrepreneur, technologist, STEM and hip hop teacher, computer programmer, and the former Director of a Code Ninjas franchise. His cross-Canada cycling tour Ride for Promise raised funds for Toronto Community Housing afterschool programs and was featured in an award-winning documentary. Curtis has been published in *CBC National News*, *Global News*, *City News*, *The Tyee*, *USPORTS*, and TEDx. In his spare time, he is a Team Canada Duathlete for the 2021 Multisport World Championships. Curtis grew up in Scarborough, Ontario, and has dedicated his life to advocating for Black and racialized youth in low-income communities in the City of Toronto and across Canada.

Curtis holds a Bachelor's in Physical and Health Education from Queen's University and a BEd in STEM education from Ontario Tech University. He has been the recipient of numerous awards including USPORTS National Russ Jackson, Herbert H. Carnegie National Citizenship, City of Toronto Spirit of Sport Diversity and Inclusion and the City of Toronto Hall of Honour inductee—winning awards alongside NBA star RJ Barrett, five-time Canadian heavyweight champion George Chuvalo, and Canadian Olympians Kylie Masse, Greg Westlake, and Stephanie Dixon.

As a self-taught computer programmer, Curtis built a mobile app which brings his memoir to life by giving readers access to hidden content that can be activated when holding your phone over photos throughout the book. He is the author and mobile app developer for the World's First Augmented Reality Memoir *Butterflies in the Trenches*. Curtis is from and lives in Scarborough.

curtiscmichael.ca 🐦📷 *@curtiscarmicc*

Curtis Carmichael is available for select speaking engagements. To inquire about possible appearances, please visit curtiscarmichael.ca for more information.

Printed in the USA
CPSIA information can be obtained
at www.ICGtesting.com
JSHW011124180224
57481JS00002B/4